Have you ever n...
the almost imposs...
carried out by men and women
who are poised and fearless,

a s k s

NORMAN VINCENT PEALE

We are constantly witnessing demonstrations of
immense human power to do what was once
considered impossible. Some people once believed
that to go beyond the atmosphere of the earth was
impossible. Today astronauts venture into space
regularly. They go without fear, never losing their
poise but with full faith in God and with full knowledge
that it is all God's universe.

This book encourages you to rediscover your identity
every single day of your life. It will help you free your
mind of apprehensions, illwill, and frustration and
realise that your potential is as limitless as the God's
universe.

The Author

Norman Vincent Peale (1898-1993) is widely acknowledged as one of the most influential clergymen of the 20th-century. He was closely indentified with the Marble Collegiate Church of Manhattan where he remained for 52 years as one of New York's most famous preachers.

Peale's simple, optimistic, and dynamic sermons were regularly broadcast, first on radio and later on television. Peale also published several best-selling books, including *The Power of Positive Thinking,* which has sold over 20 million copies and has been translated into 41 different languages, *Treasury of Courage & Confidence, Why Some Positive Thinkers Get Powerful Results, Positive Imaging, Power of The Plus Factor, Reaching Your Potential* (all in Orient Paperbacks).

In 1945, Dr. Peale, with his wife Ruth Stafford Peale, founded *Guideposts* Magazine. With little money but a strong vision, *Guideposts* was designed to be a non-denominational forum for people – both celebrities and ordinary folk – to relate their inspirational stories. Today, under the direction of Ruth Peale *Guideposts* is the 13th largest paid-circulation magazine in the US with a circulation of over 4 million.

Dr. Peale's message of positive thinking, strong faith and helping others achieve their true potential continues to live on with us well into the new millennium.

Positive Living
Day by day

NORMAN VINCENT PEALE

Orient
Paperbacks

DELHI | MUMBAI | HYDERABAD

Acknowledgments

The material by Norman Vincent Peale contained in this book is used by permission of the Peale Centre, New York, and Guideposts, New York.

www.orientpaperbacks.com

ISBN-81-222-0367-1

1st Published in Orient Paperbacks 2004

Positive Living Day by Day

© 2002 Ideals Publications

Published in arrangement with
Ideals Publications
a division of Guideposts, Nashville, USA

Cover design by Vision Studio

Published by
Orient Paperbacks
(A division of Vision Books Pvt. Ltd.)
Madarsa Road, Kashmere Gate, Delhi-110 006

Printed in India at
Rakesh Press, Delhi-110 068

Cover Printed at
Ravindra Printing Press, Delhi-110 006

Positive
Living
Day by day

THE HAMMER OF CIRCUMSTANCES

James Russell Lowell made a remark one time that has always fascinated me, he said, 'Mishaps are like knives that either serve us or cut us, as we grasp them by the blade or the handle.' If you grasp the blade of a difficulty, it will cut you; but if you grasp the handle of a difficulty, you can cut your way through all manner of obstructions.

The Russians have a proverb that I like: 'The hammer shatters the glass, but forges steel.' If you're glass, if you're superficial, if there's no faith in you, adversity will crack and shatter you. But if you have in you the victory that overcomes the world, then the hammer of circumstance hitting you forges you into a strong person. God knew what He was doing when He constructed this world so that there was difficulty in it. That is what makes it possible for us to grow in strength and understanding. There is conflict in the universe and that is what makes life go.

I AM IN CONTROL OF THIS CAR

*O*nce while in San Francisco, I climbed into one of the cable cars alongside the grip man — the man who runs it — and the car filled up with people. We were travelling down the Powell Street hill at high speed. It looked as though at each moment we were in imminent danger of destruction, but this made it a more exciting ride. I asked the grip man, 'Don't you ever get nervous when this car starts plunging down this grade?'

'Nervous?' he replied. 'Never. Because, you see, I know I'm in control of this car. So why should I be nervous?'

As we career down the steep grades of our lives, we sometimes have dark apprehensions of what may happen. But if you know you are in emotional control, you then can handle any situation. It is when we finally relax in God that we find health and well-being and deep joy.

GO HUNTING

$\mathscr{A}$n important thing to realize is that it doesn't make any difference how much difficulty there is — there are always great possibilities in any situation.

Generally, when people are disheartened, they can't see the possibilities. They see only the difficulties that are involved, not the solution. They magnify the difficulties, to blow them up, to make them bigger than they actually are.

The thing to do when you are disheartened is the very opposite: go hunting around in your situation for the bright possibilities that are surely there.

I AM SCARED TO SPEAK!

$\mathcal{S}$everal years ago, I was to speak at a dinner and was seated next to the United States Senator from New Jersey, Warren Barbour. He seemed fidgety and he surprised me by remarking, 'I'm glad you're speaking first. Having to speak still scares the wits out of me.'

'But why, if you were so afraid of speaking,' I asked him, 'did you run for public office?'

'Actually,' he confided, 'my fear of speaking was one reason I decided to run. I was determined that I wasn't going to go through life reeling because I was afraid to speak. I find that the more I do it, the less I fear it.'

You and I, when experiencing fear, should remember to have a holy boldness. I call it that because it is of God. He put potential boldness into you. We cannot do it of our own unaided strength, but with God's ever-present help, we can.

YOU AREN'T 'REALLY STUPID'

𝒯ruth is the wisdom of God in the mind and in the soul of man. So many people have so little grasp of truth that they are constantly plagued by mistakes.

A gentleman who was really concerned about himself asked me a question. As he put it, 'Why am I so dumb? Why do I do so many dumb things?'

His IQ was very high. He was a graduate of a celebrated university. But this man had lost six jobs in ten years, and in every instance it was because he did something stupid. 'Now,' he said, 'tell me what is wrong with me.'

I remarked, 'You aren't really stupid.' And I pointed him to the answer that will help anyone in that situation: 'Jim, if you will commit your life to God so that He takes over your thought processes, you will be guided and will not make all these mistakes.'

$\mathcal{S}$ome years ago I met a man named Oelroyd. He was the curator of the house in Washington, D.C., across from Ford's Theatre, to which Abraham Lincoln was carried after the assassin shot him, and where he died. Mr. Oelroyd showed me a Bible which he said had been used by Lincoln during the critical days of the Civil War. Opening it, he pointed to a verse and to a slightly soiled indentation alongside it near the edge of the page, which looked as if it might have been made by a finger. Mr. Oelroyd liked to think that this was evidence that Lincoln frequently turned to that verse, which says: 'I sought the Lord, and he answered me; he delivered me from all my fears.'

Now the psalmist doesn't say that God delivered him from some fears, but from all his fears.

LET GO!

$\mathcal{F}$or many years I never experienced an operation firsthand. But my turn came. My doctor told me he had to remove my gallbladder. On the appointed morning, I told my wife that I loved her. And she told me the same. Then I asked the Lord to forgive me for any sins that I had committed. And I thanked Him for all His goodness. I looked out at the beautiful Dutchess County hillside and I said, 'I love this world, Lord, and I'd like to go on and do a good job.'

Now this is a simple thing I'm telling you. But what I did was let go. I committed my soul to God. Have you ever really done that? It's a tremendous experience. Friends, I want to tell you that in that one minute I had an experience of the Presence. I felt a sustaining power. I had a sense of reality. And it is going to live with me all the rest of my life. You don't have to wait for an operation or an illness to commit your life to Him. You can do it now.

WALK TALL!

*P*hyllis Simolke was in New York City on a buying trip. After a happy reunion, she went with a friend to the subway and waited until a train came. Her friend got on, and they waved to each other as the train moved off. She started toward the exit. All at once, five thugs appeared and blocked her passage. The young woman froze. Mrs. Simolke had a committed faith. So she prayed to the Lord, saying, 'For the sake of my two little boys and my husband, help me.' And He did.

She walked straight up to the leader, a tall fellow with a scar on his face. Standing tall, she said gently but firmly, 'Let me pass, please.'

Like the parting of the Red Sea, they broke ranks. As she passed, one punk hissed, 'You walk tall, woman. Walk tall!' — as though in his mind there glimmered a respect for the immense power available to renewed people. Phyllis Simolke is the kind of person who lives with unchanging truth in a changing world.

THE GREAT CONTACT

$\mathcal{P}$rayer is the contact of the soul with God through the mental processes whereby the individual conquers his own weaknesses and enters into life abundant. If you have the idea that it is merely the mumbling of a few words, I almost think you're better off not to use it at all, for that is a degradation of this great process.

True prayer requires discipline, it requires pain, it requires the agony to think. But when you do think prayerfully, with God as your guide, you break free from the defeats which have encompassed you.

I do not believe there is any problem, any defeat, any difficulty that cannot be overcome through prayer. I do not believe there is any disease from which prayer cannot bring deliverance. One of the most devastating enemies of man is disease, but one reason it devastates is because we just accept it as inevitable. I believe in the power of God to resolve any difficulty, to remove any weakness, to heal any disease.

LIVE WITH COURAGE

*Y*ou may be full of fear. You have had fears all your life. You are so sick of these fears that you just don't know what to do, but you are in the habit of saying to yourself, 'I've always been a fearful person. My grandfather was a fearful person, my mother was a fearful person — so I am a fearful person. That's just the way it is. That's just the way I'm made.' What an evaluation of yourself!

Say instead: 'Dear God, I believe that You can give me power. I hereby repudiate these fears. I am from this minute on a person of courage.' Then you will go out and live with courage. You'll do things you formerly were afraid to do. You'll live dangerously. And after a while you will find that your fears are gone.

The same is true of excitement and enthusiasm. Live on the basis of enthusiasm and excitement and you'll have them. And they will make a different person out of anyone who does it.

LOVE LIVING

$\mathcal{A}$t a luncheon I was seated next to a distinguished woman who asked me what extra thing I was doing now. 'Writing a book,' I said. 'The working title is *Enthusiasm Makes the Difference*.'

'I want to congratulate you on your audacity and your courage,' she said, 'that you would actually write a book on enthusiasm in a day and age like this.'

Well, I was surprised to know that this required courage and audacity. But I shall persevere in encouraging people to sing in their spirit.

How does one have enthusiasm in his life? It is as simple as this: Cultivate the ability to love living. Love the people who live, love the sky under which you live, love the season in which we pass these days, love all of the facets of living.

The person who loves becomes happy. The person who loves everything becomes enthusiastic, filled with the zest and the joy of life. It is just that simple.

BRAVE LITTLE DAVID

*T*he story of David and Goliath might be told in this fashion: The Philistines had a giant named Goliath. He would yell at the Israelites, 'Come out and fight. If your giant defeats me, we will be your slaves; but if I defeat him, you'll be our slaves.'

David, a clear-minded boy, went to the king and said, 'If you will let me, I will take care of this fellow.' This went over well with the king. He said, 'If you want to take on the giant, you may do it.'

David collected five smooth stones and proceeded in the direction of the giant. He swung his slingshot, and the stone smacked the giant right on the forehead. And Goliath toppled over, dead.

What a story! And what does it teach? A simple truth. You are faced with a Goliath. Everybody is. But no difficulty is bigger than you are when you are united with God. Together you and God have the power to do mighty things of which you know not.

TOUGH SITUATIONS

$\mathcal{W}$hen you are up against a tough situation, the first essential is to stand up to it. Face it, think about it, study it, pray about it; then hit it and keep after it. You have within you enough force, put there by Almighty God, to overcome situations that seem overwhelming. If you practice faith constantly, if you keep in His spirit, if you stay in tune with Him, you can bring the necessary strength into play against all difficulties.

Don't ever think you're weak. Don't ever say you're weak. Don't ever believe you're weak. You're not weak. Draw upon your strength. And maybe it seems that you have very little strength, but you can bring it into play against difficulties and overcome them.

GOD IS WITH YOU

I believe a person should pray for courage as he prays for his daily bread. God will give it to you, because He will give you Himself. Let me illustrate.

At a prayer breakfast in Washington, General Harold K. Johnson, Chief of Staff of the United States Army, related an instance from his life. During the Korean War, General Johnson found himself in charge of a handful of men holding a dreary stretch of deserted road to cover a retreat.

'I was very troubled,' he said, 'so I just shut my eyes and talked to God, right there on that cold, frozen road. I asked His help. And out of the night, as if from a great distance, came God's voice saying, "Be strong, have no fear, I am with you." ' From that moment he had no fear, only a deep sense of peace. And he and his men had the courage they needed to fight their way out of that situation.

THE ULTIMATE VICTORY

$\mathcal{M}$y wife and I were in England and went to Chartwell, Winston Churchill's home where he lived during the war. Outside the house we were shown where he stood every evening during the Battle of the Britain, watching the German bombers coming over in great waves. I asked our guide, 'Did he ever lose hope?'

She laughed. 'Churchill? No. Hope was built into him. He never expected anything but ultimate victory.' That is why some men become immortal. They have hope and expectation built into him.

Well, you may think, I'm not Churchill; I'm just a plain human being. Certainly you are! But don't say you are going to let these things defeat you. Not when you have God, who will put such a glow of victory and health in you that it will be a thrill.

FAITH IS STRONGER
THAN FEAR!

The two greatest forces in the world, ceaselessly contending with each other, are fear and faith. But faith is stronger than fear.

I am reminded of a talk I had with J. Edgar Hoover, who was head of the Federal Bureau of Investigation. In his early career, he was famous for his fearless pursuit of vicious criminals. I said to him, 'When you were hunting those gangsters, were you ever afraid?'

'Of course I was afraid,' he answered. 'There were many times when I might have been shot to death at any moment. Of course I was afraid.'

'How did you overcome your fear?' I asked.

Instantly he replied: 'I lost my fear in the power of my Lord.' He added, 'Get the power of the Lord in your heart and you overcome your fear.'

SOAR HIGH

$\mathcal{I}$ consider it a travesty of the gospel of Jesus Christ to insist that there should be no expression of joy in this world. It was said of the first Christians that they had within them the song of the skylark and the babbling of brooks. But today that lilt seems, for the most part, to have gone out of Christian preaching. And this is a tragedy.

Now, of course, if you see only clouds, you naturally are not going to say, 'It's good to be alive.' But believe me, friends, there is much more in this world than clouds. And if that's all you see, then you should have a change of view-point. Take flight within yourself. It is a wonderful thing to have altitude in your thoughts. You can have it if you just take it. And altitude of the spirit makes all the difference in the world.

THE HAPPIEST PEOPLE

$\mathcal{W}$illiam Lyon Phelps, who in the early years of the twentieth century was one of the most famous of American professors at a great New England university, once wrote, 'The happiest people are those who think the most interesting thoughts.'

One morning in New York City, as I left my apartment for the day, the doorman, with a dour expression on his face, said to me, 'This is one of the most miserable days I've ever seen.'

For a moment it dashed my spirits, but I rose to the occasion and replied, 'This is the day the Lord has made; let us rejoice and be glad in it.' A new expression came over the man's face, so maybe I gave him a different idea. That's the way you've got to think. Your happiness in life depends upon how you think about everything.

How do you think about your future? Do you see it as gloomy? If you do, it will be so. Don't see it that way. See it as happy. See God in it. See God controlling your mind, and happiness will come.

THAT EXTRA SOMETHING

*Y*our mind is a powerful instrument. If it controls you, you'll not be victorious. But if you control it, you will win.

However, I don't believe that a human being by his own unaided strength can accomplish this. Something else needs to be added.

I once knew a distressed man who held steady and made his way back up with the help of a wonderful dynamic thought that changes everything. Given what little I know about human beings and about God, I will guarantee that this thought can help anybody under any circumstances to keep on keeping on. Everyone would do well to hold it in consciousness until it absorbs into the unconsciousness and live by it. This thought can be found in the Bible. And this is it: I can do all things through — myself? No. 'I can do everything through him who gives me strength.' God will help you keep on keeping on.

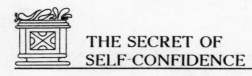

THE SECRET OF
SELF-CONFIDENCE

A university put out a questionnaire among six hundred psychology students and asked them, among other things, to reveal what they thought was their most pressing, painful, personal problem. Seventy percent of them said that it was lack of courage or self-confidence.

What, then, is the secret of self-confidence and courage? It hinges on the kinds of thoughts you think. Your subconscious is very accommodating. If you keep on sending it fearful thoughts and self-inadequacy thoughts, that is what it will feed back to you.

When you come right down to it, the secret of courage and self-confidence is to fill your life with God. Of course, you expect me to say that. And you are not going to be disappointed, because I've said it. And why do I say it? Because it's true. You were created by God and He made you right. If you haven't walked with God, you are making yourself wrong.

THE GREATEST THING
ABOUT YOU

*Y*our physical body is a marvellous instrument. Most everybody has a hand, and it seems to be an ordinary appliance. But consider the positions and motions you can make with your fingers and your hand. Think of the angles, the joints, the engineering that goes into the one small member of your body known as a hand! But your wonderful body isn't the greatest thing about you.

There is in you that indescribable thing called God's power. It is a power over yourself, a power over situations, a power over circumstance. If you exercise this power, amazing things can be done with it. Now you must be humble about it. It isn't your power. It is God living within you. This is why we constantly urge people to come into a closer relationship with God. Because what does He do? He releases power whereby anyone can transform himself or herself.

EVERYTHING IS POSSIBLE

I call to your attention a text in the New Testament. And it is probably one of the greatest gems of truth you will find. It says: 'Everything is possible for him who believes.'

Notice that there is a condition. You are offered something tremendous, but only if you have faith. In-depth belief requires giving your whole self to it. It isn't the glib recital of a creed. But if you can overcome your doubts and your negative thinking and really, deeply believe, you will enter into a life transformed. This is the magic of believing. Belief is factual; it is truth.

The magic of believing is a manifestation of one of the greatest powers in the universe: the power of thought. By our thoughts we either create or destroy. You can tear your life down by destructive thinking, but you can build your life up by thinking constructively.

WISDOM OF GOD

We live in the midst of the greatest scientific civilization in the history of the world. But the greatest wisdom walking our streets is not that of any laboratory scientist, but the wisdom of God. When you have to solve perplexing problems and handle tough situations, He will give you the calm, quiet, orderly mind without which no solution can emerge. So the first thing is: don't panic. The second thing is: think. That's what God enables a person to do. He teaches you to think.

Write all the parts of the problem out. Talk it over with people whose intelligence and understanding you respect. Then do something about it. Do anything you can think of to find an answer. And never, never give up. Because there is an answer, and in God's leading, you will be guided to the answer if you keep on thinking, keep on working at it.

MONEY, DIPLOMACY AND GOD

What is the hope of the world? Is it in the military? Is it in money? Is it in diplomacy? I would say that the diplomacy of the world hasn't succeeded too well, although without it we might be worse off by far than we are. Military force will never save the world. Education won't save it either. If all the people in the world are able to read, that is not going to guarantee anything, because what will they read?

I tell you, the hope of the world is in God, because He alone can bridge the gap between people. He alone can establish a fellowship that is basic. He alone brings people together as brothers. Under Him, you no longer see people's race, nor their colour, nor their background, nor their present condition; you see only a human soul, a child of God. If we could just get this world full of God.

ELEVATING EXPERIENCES

*P*art of having meaning in your life is to get lifted out of yourself, to get high, so to speak. Everybody needs a high experience once in awhile. You can't live adequately without great experiences. You must have great experiences at intervals. For instance, you can be caught up by some great music or be lifted by some beauty in nature or have some marvellous experience of love with other human beings. You need these elevated experiences. For instance, Jesus said, 'I have come that they may have life, and have it to the full'. In other words, that we might have it high — have meaning in your life.

NEW START

$\mathscr{E}$veryone wants to make a new start. How can this be done? The formula is very simple. One sentence gives the answer to the whole matter. Put this thought at the centre of your consciousness, stay with it, and you will keep it right every day: 'I am the light of the world. Whoever follows me will never walk in darkness, but will have the light of life.'

How many more years do you think you are going to have? Are you going to have fifty more? Thirty more? Ten more? One more? Very seldom does anybody have more than one hundred. Most people do not even have as many as eighty-five. It would seem that since we have so few years, we ought to figure out what is the best procedural wisdom to apply to them. I believe it is contained in the text, 'I am the light of the world. Whoever follows me will never walk in darkness, but will have the light of life.'

THE POWER OF PRAYER

$\mathcal{H}$oward M. LeSourd was a dean of one of the colleges of Boston University. He is not emotional about religion, yet he brings God into the little activities of life. He wrote me a note saying. 'Thank you for the Sunday morning services, which have brought comfort and inspiration to us,' and went on to tell of this incident: 'Last night our car stalled on Forty-second Street. It would not start.' His wife began to pray for help. 'When she opened her eyes, a man ws standing by the car saying "If you have a pair of pliers, I think I can help you." I produced the pliers. He raised the hood, released the choke, and the engine started immediately.' Isn't God wonderful?

This is a very simple illustration, but God always has His eyes on you. He notes the fall of a sparrow; even the very hairs of your head are numbered. So He is big enough to be interested in everyday human life.

THINK BIG, BELIEVE BIGGER

$\mathcal{Y}$ears ago, a member of Marble Collegiate Church played guard on the Northwestern University football team. Apparently he wasn't exerting himself to the fullest, for the coach kept him back one day and told him, 'You have it in you to be the greatest guard Northwestern ever had. But you've got to think bigger than you're thinking; you've got to believe bigger than you're believing.' He added something the man says he never forgot — and which I have never forgotten since he told me. 'Okay boy,' said the coach, 'go out there on the field running tall.' What a phrase!

So I urge you as I urge myself: Get out there on the field running tall, thinking big, believing big, setting your goals high enough for the good that Almighty God has created for you. Think that good, believe that good, work for that good.

CAN YOU MAKE CANDY?

I once met a lady who lives in Mississippi who said, 'I thought my husband would provide for me so that when he died I needn't worry. But his estate was eaten up, and I've got to go to work or go on relief.'

I didn't know what to suggest. So I prayed, 'Lord, give us an insight for Miss Lou.' At the end of the prayer I hit on it. I asked, 'Can you make candy?'

'Now that is something I can do,' she answered.

'You go home,' I said, 'and make me a pound of it. Send it to me.'

Actually she sent me a two-pound box and it was marvellous candy. So I wrote her saying. 'Get busy merchandising that candy.'

If you go to Edwards, Mississippi, you will find a shop there called 'The Sweetest Spot.' Miss Lou found that by thinking creatively, she could change her life. And by serving others, she became a great influence for good in the area where she lives.

GOD'S HARD REFUSALS

God in His wisdom isn't going to give you and me everything we want, because He knows what we need. I am reminded of Rabindranath Tagore, the great Indian mystic and poet, who said, 'I have often been saved by God's hard refusals.'

Not getting something you greatly desire isn't pleasant. It can be painful. It can be very bitter. But sometimes the greatest thing that ever happens to us is when God says, 'No. I want it another way.' Infantile people complain and say that God is cruel or that there is no God. Mature people, however, know there is wisdom and sometimes an eternal kindness in God's refusals.

GET EXCITED ABOUT LIFE

$\mathcal{H}$ave you ever gotten excited about life itself? Are you ever thrilled by the mere fact that you are alive? It is a great thing to be alive. It means that you can feel, you can sense, you can dream, you can think, you can love, you can have relationships with other people.

Yes, it's a great thing to be alive. But there are lots of people walking around who are only half-alive. Yet they can come alive. You can come alive right now, today. You can throw off all your darkness, your dullness, your dreariness, your negativism, and really live, if you open your mind and heart and receive God.

HEALTH AND HAPPINESS

$\mathcal{N}$ot long ago, I saw a man whom I hadn't seen for a while. When I first knew him, he seemed to be only half alive and complained continually of not feeling well. At one time, he had a partial nervous breakdown. When I saw him later, I could hardly believe it was the same man. He had come alive.

His method consists of spending fifteen minutes every day filling his mind full of God. And how do you go about it? You think about God, you read or repeat to yourself scriptural statements about God, you talk to Him, you let Him bring you into a God-centred state of mind. Health and happiness are available to everyone. But they are gifts of God, for He is the source of health and happiness.

STORY OF HOPE

$\mathscr{A}$ woman tells this story of hope: 'During the Depression, we had a terrible time. Only my married daughter's help — which she could ill afford — was keeping us alive. Things got to a point where I even thought of suicide as a way out. Then I thought, "If I can depend on my daughter's love, why can't I depend on God's?" I got down on my knees, telling God I would leave everything in His hands. Then I prayed for those whose actions I had resented because they had injured us. And I arose from that prayer with joy in my heart.

'The next day my husband got temporary work. I went back to college to get my degree so I could teach. And it wasn't long before my husband had a permanent job and I became a regular teacher. We gradually paid off all our debts. When my husband was incapacitated, we were able to retire on pension.

'My own strength was not enough, but when I admitted it to God and put myself in His care, His strength was made perfect in my weakness.'

START ANOTHER STREAM

One of the worst things you can do is to permit a continuous trickle of worry across the mind, because like water it will ultimately dig a huge trench. Then every thought you think will be drained into this channel of fear and worry and come up tinctured with anxiety. You will be a person full of fear and worry.

The way to obliterate this is to start another stream. Let a stream of faith run across the mind and go deeper and deeper as you absorb faith thoughts into your consciousness — and after a while it will undercut the channel of fear and worry which will then fall into the channel of faith, and a great river of faith will surge through your mind so that every thought will come up bright and resplendent, optimistic and hopeful, and life will be good, very good. Cultivate a channel of faith to give you the deep security which you need.

THE ONE LETTER DIFFERENCE

You may constantly think *scarcity*. I have observed that people who think scarcity tend in a strange way to manifest scarcity. The word scarcity is related to the word scarce. And there is only one letter difference between scarce and scare. It could be that if you think scarcity you scare money and prosperity away. This is, as I say, a little harder to demonstrate than the other correlations between attitudes and outcomes, but you might consider trying it out. Instead of saying, 'How difficult everything is for me; how poor I am,' affirm how God is helping you, how blessed you are. Avoid manifesting scarcity by avoiding scarcity thoughts.

By the same token, if in our minds we entertain thanksgiving, we manifest blessings. The more thankfulness a person cultivates, the more, I do believe, he will open to himself the power flow, the vast wealth of heaven, and blessings will pour out upon him.

DO YOU FOLLOW THROUGH?

*S*ome time ago I received a telephone call from a stranger who said, 'I heard your talk tonight. I'm having a bad time. I know that my main problem is myself, but what I want to ask is, will you pray for me?'

'Of course,' I said. 'And I will do it right now.' When I concluded the prayer, his reverent 'Amen' echoed my own. After a moment he said, 'Thanks a lot. I will get busy and follow through on that prayer.'

When he had hung up, I asked myself: Do I follow through on my prayers? How often have I prayed 'gimme' kind of prayers or desperation kind of prayers or bewildered prayers with no results? Having prayed, do I believe God has heard? Do I leave it with Him? Or do I shut out answers by continuing to expect the worst? Do I try to do something about the thing myself? I think everyone could ask these same questions. When you pray, do you follow through?

TOUGH MINDED AND OPTIMISTIC

I have a letter from a woman who told me that if I wished to share her story I could. Here is what she says:

'They tell me I have heart disease and only one year to live. I don't believe they always know, especially about us Irish Christians, who are made of pretty tough stuff! I have buried two sons. I've had nine operations and rheumatic fever, in addition to this heart disease. You're probably thinking, "That poor woman!" But don't you dare. Save your pity for some poor soul who isn't tough-minded and optimistic.

'I'm forty-five years young and I'm going to live to be ninety if the Lord wills it. I've never been in need since I found the Lord. I'm proud that God has chosen me to bear these crosses, and grateful that He gave me a strong back to bear them.

'I'm happy. My friends tell me I'm a character. I'm never quite sure just how they mean it. But if I'm a character because I can laugh and enjoy God's wonderful world we live in, then I'm a character.'

THE FIVE RULES

I believe that faithful following of these five rules will revolutionize the life of any person.

First: Be bold, and mighty forces will come to your aid. The person who is afraid cuts himself off from the flow of power, but when you venture boldly, there comes a flow of power in response.

Second: Deny adverse conditions. Don't go around saying or thinking: 'Conditions are against me.' Face facts, but realize that it often happens that a person is defeated not so much by the facts of a situation as by his negative interpretation of the facts. In every problem there is an inherent good. Believe that.

Third: Picture good outcomes. By envisioning good things, you actually bring good influences into play, both within yourself and in the world around you.

Fourth: Pray for every person you meet with by name, that he or she may benefit from the dealings you have with him or her.

Fifth: Practice love toward everybody.

MORE THAN CONQUERORS

*W*hen you have experienced a defeat, you should promptly make a new endeavour. Otherwise you'll get the idea that life's too much for you and will keep defeating you. When you experience a defeat, say, 'Lord, I messed this one up badly.'

He'll say to you, 'Just take more of Me into your heart and into your life.'

That's the message which poor, defeated humanity needs to hear and heed. You cannot handle everything with just your own strength. But with God, we become 'more than conquerors.' He will not let us be tempted beyond our strength, which means we shall be equal to any circumstances or conditions we may encounter. And if we stay in contact with God, we continue to receive this power.

MONEY TROUBLES

$\mathscr{A}$ couple consulted a minister in California and said, 'We don't understand why we have money trouble all the time. You talk about the boundless generosity of God, but we never see anything of it.' And they asked, 'Will you pray for us?'

The minister gave them a strange task. 'Tomorrow I want you to go to the beach. See if you can calculate how many grains of sand the Lord made. When you get tired of considering the sand, walk through the park and count all the leaves on the trees.

'I want you to realize,' the minister told them, 'that this God who has put all the sand on the beach and all the leaves on the trees is trying to put blessings into your life. But you're closed. Your belief is too little.'

The couple went and talked it over with God. And they began to re-appraise their lives. They started an enterprise that brought new value and prosperity to their lives. They learned to believe big, pray big, think big, and built themselves a full, rich, satisfying life.

THE GREATEST FACT

*G*od will help you if you let Him. Even God, with all His power, cannot help you unless you will allow Him to do so, for He has made man a free agent, with power of choice. But one of the greatest of all facts is that God is ever-ready to help you with whatever difficulty you may have, however great it may be. With His help, you will either solve your problem, overcome your difficulty, or learn to live with it and get along with it.

Take any sizable group of people and you can find the whole range of human problems represented to one degree or another among them. There will be people who are very sad, labouring under a weight of grief; there will be people who are very discouraged, for whom things haven't gone well, who have encountered much resistance and to whom life seems very hard. But God will help them all if they will let Him.

A MAN NAMED FORD PHILPOT

*O*nce in Miami Beach, I spoke to a large audience of businessmen. Among those present was a man named Ford Philpot, who was one of the greatest demonstrations of will power I have ever encountered. Ford was a young man with all kinds of personality, but he had become an alcoholic. In the grip of that complicated disease, he sank lower and lower. He was expelled from school and spent all his time in bars.

Everybody — family, friends, doctors, everybody — had tried to help him, but with no success. Then one night he unaccountably decided to reach for a power that could save him. Later the same night, he knelt in prayer with a group of dedicated men, and by midnight, was so completely delivered from his old weakness that it never again controlled him. He became a minister who helped and inspired many other human beings.

STAND UP TO YOUR PROBLEM

*Y*ou don't have to stand up to your problem alone, for God is with you. And this is really a great thing. If we had to stand up to tough problems alone, life would be very bitter. In the end, it would be a losing battle, for man isn't that big. The greatest among us is small in the presence of some problems of human life. So we should forever be mindful and grateful, that we are not alone.

The secret, then, is to stand up to your problem by taking it and doing all you can about it. Then put it in God's hands, turning it over to Him. Turn away from the problem and turn to God. When you pick the problem up again, it will be the way He wants it. And that means it will be right. You'll get your answer. It may be 'no,' it may be 'wait a while,' it may be 'yes,' but it will be the right answer.

IN THE TEMPLE OF SILENCE

I was on friendly terms with Jesse L. Lasky, a pioneer of the motion picture industry and a wonderful and spiritually minded man. One evening at his home, he said to me, 'Before dinner I want you to spend fifteen minutes in my silence room.' I was intrigued, of course.

He took me to a room used as a place to practice creative silence. On the table there was a Bible and a stack of cards on which he had written texts from the Bible which had to do with silence and peace.

'I will leave you here,' he said, 'to commune with God's silence.' He was gone for fifteen minutes. It was a delightful, renewing experience.

Are you aware of inner silence even now? You can spend this very moment in the temple of silence, acquainting yourself with God and becoming peaceful. Practice creative silence.

THE PROBLEM OF FEAR

There are plenty of people who experience fear continually without even having any notion what it is they are afraid of. Now, what can you do about the problem of fear? You can do either one of two things. One is to give in to your fears and permit yourself to be dominated by them all your life. Many people do just that. They carry their fears with them all the days of their lives, suffering misery and inner conflict until the very end of their days. That is a piteous thing.

The other course — the only alternative — is to rise up in the full stature of your manhood or womanhood and, with all the help of Almighty God, dominate your fears. If you do that, you will have gained a victory that will make you worthy of eternal life. That kind of greatness is possible in every human being.

FIND THE ANSWER

$\mathcal{A}$ man once gave me an insight into overcoming problems. 'My mother,' he told me, 'used to say, "When you have a problem and you've worked as hard as you can at it and still haven't solved it, the thing to do is just walk away and think about God. But don't talk to God about the problem. Tell Him how much you love Him, thank Him for all He has done for you, tell Him you want to be His faithful follower. Have fellowship with God." '

How wise that woman was! An irreligious person might advise you to put the problem aside and play a game of golf. But there is a vast difference between playing a game of golf and talking to God — God lifts you way up, so that when you go back to the problem you have grown, the problem has shrunk. Then, Prayerfully, you can break it open and find the answer.

LAW OF SUPPLY

$\mathcal{I}$ recall the wisdom of the man from whom I first heard of the law of supply. He went through fire and flood and depression and panic and made out all right. He used to say, 'The law of supply never failed me once.'

'What is this "law of supply"?' I asked him. I had never heard of it in the school I went to.

'It is an inclination of the universe to sustain you if you're in harmony with the flow of rightness. And you get in harmony with it by letting your thoughts open up big. Let the soul flower out,' he said. 'Speak big, pray big, ask big, give big, believe big, love big, and bigness will flow to you.'

Now this doesn't mean that by being in harmony with the law of supply, you will necessarily get rich. God isn't going to line your pockets, but He will give you all you need if you are in harmony with His will, loving and serving others and forgetting yourself — in other words, if your soul gets big.

GET AWAY FROM YOURSELF

$\mathcal{I}$ was reading in the Gospel of Luke about the time when Jesus told his disciples to launch out into deep water if they wanted to get any fish. It's a message to anyone who wants to pack meaning into his life. Get away from yourself. Don't be tied up with yourself. Don't hang on to yourself. 'Put out into deep water, and let down the nets for a catch' — and you'll pull up more values than you could imagine.

One of the ways you launch out into the deep is to embrace the profound principle that abiding, joyous life comes only through giving. The people who throw themselves into some great social issue — forgetting themselves, being willing to suffer hurt if necessary for their convictions and ideals — become the happiest people in the world because they are growing bigger. When you give, you get bigger, you grow, your personality expands. You become a far greater individual by giving yourself, your time, your money.

FEER OF DECISION MAKING

$\mathcal{M}$any years ago the president of a great corporation told me, 'For years I have made decisions on problems and made them fast. Now I live in fear of making decisions. You're a spiritual doctor. Can you give me a prescription to cure me of this?'

So I gave him this prescription: 'When you get up in the morning, say, "Thank you, Lord, for giving me a good night's sleep. Now I'm going to go to work. And each time I have to make a decision, I'm going to talk with You about it. I can't go wrong with You helping me." Before you go to sleep say, "Thank You, Lord, for all the decisions we made today."'

He assured me he would follow the prescription. And he did. He became a strong, effective man again, having discovered that if you seek the Lord, He will hear you and will deliver you from all your fears.

A VITAL INGREDIENT

*C*onfidence is a vital ingredient of living. The Bible regards confidence — faith in God — as necessary to our well-being. One day you may notice a huge obstacle in your pathway. You can't get around it and you don't know what to do about it. That is your mountain. It has you licked. But you can knock it down if you have faith, if you believe.

You can overcome gigantic obstacles and have a life more wonderful than you ever imagined if you recondition your mind. Learn to reject small thinking. Never admit a negative thought. Never give utterance to defeatist fears. Talk it up, think it up, believe it up! As you think big, big results will come.

OUT OF A LITTLE CELL

*A*fter a speech one evening, a young man told me his story: 'I was a salesman, but I couldn't sell,' he said in a booming voice. 'I knew the trouble was that I had clamps on me of shyness and self-doubt. These things held me tight and I couldn't get free. I went to my pastor and he said, "Bill, turn to Jesus and ask Him to free you of these things. If you give your life to the Lord, He will give Himself to you."

'So,' Bill said, 'I did and those clamps fell away, and I was able to sell. But I realized that the big thing that had happened was that I was free inside. It was as if I had moved out of a little cell into the big wide world.'

The man's face glowed. People who stood listening had misty eyes, for they were seeing one of the greatest things in the world: a man set free by the power of God.

THE PROFOUND LAW OF HUMAN NATURE

There is a very profound law of human nature which says that we become, to a very large degree, what we think.

If you think little and believe little and act little, the results are likely to be little. If, on the other hand, you think big, believe big, and act big, the results are very likely to equate with bigness.

Religious thought is far greater than anyone realizes. It tells weak people that they can become strong. It tells defeated people that they can become victorious. It tells unhappy, mixed-up people that they can become organized. It teaches that we can become great. There is nothing else like it in the whole wide world.

LIVE BY YOUR FAITH

$\mathscr{A}$ man wandering outside on a moonless night decided to take a shortcut through the cemetery. He stepped in some loose dirt and fell to the bottom of a newly dug grave. He tried to climb out but couldn't, so he decided to just take it easy until morning.

He was half asleep when a second man slipped in the dirt and also fell into the grave. He struggled to get out and couldn't. In the darkness, the first man said, 'You'll never get out of this grave.' But the second man, startled, did get out. Fear sent him over the top.

Faith, however, is an even greater force. A ball will roll downhill, a flower will come out of a seed, and faith will cancel out fear. So the secret we must all master, if our lives are to be as effective as we want them to be, is how to get our faith built up, how to protect it, how to live by it.

YOU CAN OVERCOME

Fear is tenacious. It gets down into the intricacies of your consciousness. So how can you get it out? The first step is to know that fear, like every other deficiency of human personality, is removable. God didn't give it to you. You took it on yourself or it was put upon you by your environment. But it is removable.

Don't think that you've got to live with fear. Don't imagine that because your father or your mother had it, or your grandfather had it, you've got to have it. You only have to have what you're willing to have. If you want to live with fear, you can. But it is removable.

Once you know that it is removable, then comes the process of removing it. And this involves something which isn't very popular with this generation, but which this generation needs to relearn: self-discipline. You can do anything you want to with yourself if you have what it takes to discipline yourself.

LIFE GLORIOUS

$\mathcal{W}$ould you like to have a sense of well-being? Would you like to be filled with energy, vitality, eagerness, enthusiasm, even excitement? That is a healthy person. How enthusiastic are you? How thrilled are you? How excited are you?

One January night, I looked out the window at midnight to see a glorious snowstorm. I became so excited that I rushed back to the bedroom where my wife was sound asleep and said, 'Ruth, get out of that bed. Let's get dressed and take a walk in the snow!'

Don't get to the point where you do not thrill to feel blood surging through your system. Don't get so you cannot breathe pure cold air down into your lungs and feel sheer exhilaration. Don't become withdrawn. Live with vitality and energy and excitement.

Life is a big word. And one of the things life includes is to have the blessings of health, to be a whole, integrated, organized, enthusiastic human being.

INTEGRITY

$\mathcal{T}$he Democratic convention that nominated Grover Cleveland for president declared, 'We love him for the enemies he has made.' During the campaign, advisers kept reminding Cleveland that, in order to be elected, he would have to carry New York state. When his campaigning brought him to New York City, he attended a dinner at which two bosses of the notorious Tammany Hall political machine were present.

After dinner these men wanted to know, 'What will you give us?' 'I will not give you one single, solitary thing,' Cleveland answered. The Tammany Hall bosses respected Cleveland's bluntness and integrity. They got behind him and helped him carry New York.

In a similar way, the presence of God helps us resist fear and intimidation. You are not alone in this great big universe. God is with you. You can stand in the presence of difficulties, pain, onslaughts, resistance, criticism, anything, and not be afraid. God is with you.

ENTHUSIASM!

$\mathcal{I}$'ve noticed that the non-enthusiast, the pessimist, has a remarkably high score for faulty judgment. For example, in 1806, William Pitt, one of the greatest statesmen in history, declared, 'There is scarcely anything around us but ruin and despair.' In 1852, the Duke of Wellington, on his deathbed, stated, 'I think God I shall be spared from seeing the consummation of ruin that is gathering about us in this world.'

Well, friends, do these comments strike you as familiar? Some people spend their lives insisting that the world is going to pieces. But the world blunders along, striving for something nobler. And the world will attain it if it keeps enthusiasm working for it. *Enthusiasm!* It is a word that is built deeply into the victorious spirit of humans. Enthusiasm literally means 'full of God.' God will help you overcome all difficulties, all tragedies, all sorrows, all heartaches, all defeats, and will give victory.

GREATEST POWER IN THE WORLD

There is no power in the world equal to spiritual power. Some people think atomic power is the greatest power in the world. Well, it is certainly an enormous, explosive power — there is no getting around that. It is a terrible power. But call to mind the sight of spring sunshine streaming through a window. There is more power there than there is in atomic energy — within a period of a few weeks, the earth awakens to that power and soon grass and flowers cover the earth, powered by something that makes no noise. That is more than atomic power can do. Just think about it. Don't judge power by the noise it makes. Judge it by the results it achieves.

...BECAUSE HE WAS LAZY

In 1907 Frank Bettger was playing baseball for Johnstown, Pennsylvania. One day, the manager fired Bettger because he was too lazy. The manager said, 'Whatever you do next, for heaven's sake, put some enthusiasm into your work.'

Bettger took the first job he could get, playing in a fourth-class league. He decided to begin acting enthusiastic, and this had an interesting result. An old ballplayer perceived that this boy had possibilities and persuaded New Haven, Connecticut, to give him a try, 'From the minute I appeared on the field,' Bettger would say, 'I acted like a man electrified.'

The next day the newspaper said, 'This new player is a barrel of enthusiasm.' They nicknamed him 'Pep' Bettger. From there he went on to big league baseball, playing third base for the St. Louis Cardinals.

'I AM NOT AFRAID'

$\mathcal{W}$e modern, civilized people live in a fear-ridden world. What things are we afraid of? We are afraid of money problems, of the boss, of the job; we are afraid of other people; we are afraid of ourselves — afraid that we will not have what it takes to do what we ought to do.

Children are afraid of their parents and, heaven help us, parents today are oftentimes afraid of their children. There is a veritable plague of fears concerning health. We are afraid of cancer, of viruses, of being awakened in the middle of the night and having to be hurried off to the hospital.

As you go about your day, say to yourself, 'I am strong in the Lord. I am not afraid. "For God did not give us a spirit of timidity, but a spirit of power, of love and of self-discipline." '

THE GREAT ACT

$\mathcal{P}$erhaps you've read the story about John Wesley, the famous religious leader, who came from England to Georgia in the eighteenth century, on a small ship. They encountered an enormous storm and Wesley, by his own admission later, was petrified.

There was a group of religious people on board, known as Moravians. They were calm and unaffected by the storm. When it was all over, Wesley asked the Moravian leader, 'How did you manage to have such composure and such faith? How can I have faith?'

The man told him, 'Act as though you have faith, and by and by, you will have faith.'

So if you want to have enthusiasm, say to yourself, 'The Lord God gave me enthusiasm. But this thing that God built into me has somehow escaped me. I know that potentially I have it. Therefore, I will act as though I were enthusiastic.' By and by, that which God gave you at birth will reassert itself.

THE SECOND COLLECTION

Sometimes when I stand at the pulpit and look out at the congregation, I could almost swear that everybody present is inwardly confident and calm. But I know that if you could gather together all the fears lurking behind all those impassive faces, you would have a great load of fear.

I've often thought it would be wonderful if we could have two collections at each church service. The first would be the usual collection of money. Then I would ask everybody to come up and lay his fears on the altar and leave them there with God. Or maybe we could have the ushers go down the aisles and take up all the fears. Then I would say, 'Let's stand and sing.' Nobody would have to be told what to sing. Everybody would feel so free and released that the whole congregation would burst out singing 'Praise God from whom all blessings flow...' so joyously it would knock off the church roof.

OPEN YOUR MIND UP

*W*hy are you depressed? Why are you discouraged? Isn't it because your mind is full of shadows, full of gloom, full of ghosts? Most fears are ghosts, and they build up in the mind. I venture that if I could open your mind, I would cut through layer after layer of gloom and doubt and darkness. Maybe that is what we ought to do with our minds at very frequent intervals — open them up.

It's too bad, really, that we have such thick skulls. What the mind needs is ventilation to let out all the dark shadows. Naturally, you can't go around cutting holes in your head, but through the use of creative thought and prayer, you can ventilate you mind. How would you feel right now if every dark shadow and apprehension were lifted out of your mind? Why, let me tell you, people would meet you and they would say, 'What in the world has come over you?' and you would be so excited and alive that you could scarcely contain yourself.

AFFIRM LIFE

$\mathcal{I}$ follow the line of thought given to me by a gentleman I knew who was told by a competent doctor that he could not live more than a year. The doctor said, 'There isn't anything specifically wrong with you, and yet everything seems to be wrong with you. Your whole organism seems to be deteriorating, and I believe it will give out within a year unless you get a tremendous infusion of faith into your mind. Affirm life. Say to yourself, "I affirm that life is operating in me. Life is going through my nerves, my bloodstream; life is in me. I shall live by the life that is from God." ' The man took the doctor's advice and recovered from his illness.

Some cynics may say, 'I don't believe in all that.' Well, that is okay by me. The man I refer to is still alive and he does believe in it. Whatever works is legitimate, if it's in harmony with the will of God. In any case, many medical professionals today believe that the cultivation of harmony between the spirituality of man and his physical being is the future of healing.

BE GLAD

$\mathcal{W}$hen you think of the world — how evil it seems to have become, how the old standards seem to have broken down, how mankind has reverted to the filth of Roman Empire days and wallows in it — remember also that there are beautiful mountains and rushing rivers and sounding seas and magnificent forests. Remember that the stars come nightly to the sky and that the sun still goes down in the west in radiant beauty.

Remember also that there are good people — people reaching for the good, people who will not let anything overwhelm them, people who see the surging fountains of the waters of life and wash themselves in them and become clean, fresh, and restored. Be glad that you have life. It is a precious thing. It is awfully good. Keep it good as long as you have it.

PRACTICE PAYS

*O*n the old days, Syracuse University had one of the greatest crew teams in the United States. Freshmen would watch them on the lake and they would go out for crew. The coach, Jim Ten Eyck, had them meet him at the football stadium. 'You see all those aisles going up and down between the seats?' he would say. 'I want you to walk up and down every one of those aisles.' When they protested, he said, 'You can't row until you've got good solid legs. You've got to have good lungs, lots of wind, deep diaphragms. You've got to be able to think too. I'll teach you how to think later on.'

A man who had rowed on one of Jim's crews told me, 'It paid off. I'll never forget the day when we pulled ahead of every other crew and won. We broke through into that power because we had practiced the work and the thinking and the discipline.'

COMING OUT ON TOP

$\mathcal{H}$ow deeply do we believe? Do we just believe superficially, without depth or commitment?

I remember talking to a celebrity years ago. I knew that she had had a great deal of trouble in her life. I asked, 'How come you keep at it with such enthusiasm?'

'Why,' she answered, 'because I love it. I give my whole self to it.' And she did; she threw everything she had into it. If you give yourself with all your heart to your business, to your children, to your marriage, to your future, to your hopes, you are going to come out with something that is lasting and strong.

THINKING TRUTH

*O*ne time I crossed the Atlantic during hurricane season. I was lying in bed, seasick, and feeling helpless as the ship pitched mercilessly. Suddenly the door opened and a cheery fellow popped in. 'What are you lying there for?' he said. 'Let's go up on deck.'

Well, that shamed me into it. We went up on deck and it was glorious. The waves were like horses with white manes thrown back. The wind drove streams of spray at us. My friend exclaimed, 'Isn't this great?'

'It really is!' I agreed. I wasn't seasick at all after that. 'You were lying there thinking error,' observed my friend, 'and up here you're thinking truth.'

I realize there are serious diseases that may be difficult to handle in this way. Yet I have seen evidence that if you don't limit the power available to you, but allow it to move up and up, you can achieve tremendous results. Remember that you are called to be a disciple and to take power and authority over all devils and cure diseases — within you as well as in others.

DAMMED-UP ANXIETY

A physician once told me that he was convinced that countless thousands of people are ill from what he called 'dammed-up anxiety.' When anxiety can't find any outlet, it infects a person's whole psychology and his whole physical condition.

There is, however, healing in God's touch. If you want to get on top of your worries for good, you can do it best by surrendering your life to God, by identifying yourself with Him, and by giving your all to Him and having that most glorious of all experiences in this world, a spiritual experience.

People afflicted with discouragement, weakness, sickness, sinfulness, hate, prejudice, and fear have found a cure in the touch of God. Say, 'Dear Lord, You take me, I take You.' And in this partnership comes healing.

THE GREAT DISCOVERY

$\mathcal{Y}$ears ago I was asked to speak to a gathering of advertising and sales people, a very sophisticated and dynamic audience. I remarked to the man who was sitting on my right that I felt power in the room. I thought it must be from the quality of those people.

'Oh,' he said, 'don't be so sure. I've been praying for this meeting.' This remark startled me; I hadn't expected to encounter such ardour.

The man then said to me, 'I found two things in life that have made everything different for me. The first — and it was the greatest single experience I ever had — was finding God and committing my life to Him. The second was that I learned to pray. These two things revolutionized my life.'

This is what Jesus has been saying to us through the years. Really astute people make this discovery. God can change your life. Prayer can change your life.

KEEP DREAMING

*W*hat do you want? See it clearly in your mind. Then check it with God; for if it isn't right, it's wrong, and no wrong thing ever turned out right. Then believe, and you will create.

You want a happy life? You want a useful life? You want to be a part of the movements of our time for human good? Do you want to rise above all your sins, weaknesses, and fears? Faith will lead you on because faith leads to belief and belief creates. Have faith in the Lord and you will be established.

Keep dreaming dreams, having visions, having faith, and you'll create. Faith also helps in another way, by taking out of us that which holds us back. I tell you right now, on the authority of God's Word — and you can check it later on — that if you do a wrong thing, you will get a wrong result. But if you let God take wrong out of you, take fear out of you, and hate out of you, He will put life into you.

LEARNING FROM MISTAKES

There is an old truism that says that we learn by our mistakes. And sometimes this is the case. But you also may reinforce a dangerous tendency: If you concentrate upon being educated by your mistakes, you may dwell on them too much. You may come to believe that making mistakes is the only teacher you have. Instead, whenever you make a mistake, you should extract from it all the know-how it may offer and then put it immediately out of your mind.

THE WORLD IS YOUR OYSTER

&ach of us was born a baby — that is the only way we get into this world — and when God gives life to a baby, He does a wonderful thing: He wraps up this adorable little package and packs him or her full to overflowing with enthusiasm. It is the one thing that characterizes an infant.

Life is thrilling, exciting, and fabulous for a baby. The world is his oyster. He simply loves it. Everything is fresh and vital. Everything is fascinating and glorious. He has the time of his life. It's too bad, isn't it, that we cannot remain as babies? The writer Huxley said that the spirit of genius is to carry the attitude of the child into old age: to keep perpetual enthusiasm.

GOOD MORNING!

𝒯he attitude you take toward the day — when the day begins — determines the day. You may wake up and say to yourself, or to the people near you, 'Oh, this is going to be a tough day. This is going to be one of the worst days I've ever been through. I can just feel it coming.' And you may find that you are absolutely right, because you are bringing it on yourself.

But if you are a person of prayer, the first thing you will do in the morning is to thank God that He watched over you and your loved ones during the night and brought you to the light of another day with all its opportunity. God gave you this day and it is a day to rejoice in.

In the course of my life, I have often observed that the more spiritually minded a person is, the more beautiful the day becomes and the more replete with opportunity it is. So if you want to have a good day every day, get your life changed by God. Then every day will be a great one.

WHY ASK FOR ANYTHING?

$\mathcal{I}$ was in a meeting not long ago where participants were talking about various difficulties and problems, both in our society and as individuals. They called upon a man to pray. I knew this man had experienced much difficulty and even then was experiencing much; and I was astonished by his prayer. He did not ask the Lord for a single thing except for His presence. And the man quickly affirmed His presence.

The prayer was full of giving of thanks and of affirmation of God's goodness. It was an entrancing prayer and I said to him, 'Jim, I know something of the difficulties you face. How come you never ask God for anything?'

'Oh,' he replied, 'I've learned that the best way to pray is to thank God. He knows what I need. Why should I ask Him for anything? Let me just tell you all the wonderful things I have.' And he began to enumerate his blessings.

No matter how much difficulty you have, and there may be much, you still have many, many things for which to be thankful.

REINVENT YOURSELF

 ne of the main principles of the Japanese religion Tenrikyo is that disease begins in the mind and if you get your mind clean, you'll be at peace, happy, creative, an asset to society.

I especially like the way they have constructed their temples. Each altar is open to the elements. The rain falls on it, the snow falls on it, the wind blows on it, the sun shines on it. Everything — rain, snow, wind, and sun — is a cleansing agent, and the lesson is that if you let the rain and snow and wind and sun of the good God into your mind, He will cleanse you of that which destroys your peace of mind.

This same idea reaches its glorious fulfilment in every religion. Not only does it cleanse, but it makes old creatures new. I've seen defeated people become victorious people, soiled people become clean people, dull people become excited. God doesn't merely create you, He repeatedly re-creates you.

GET ATTACHED

T.E.Lawrence once took some Arabs to London; what interested them more than anything else were the faucets in the bathrooms in their hotel. They would turn the water on and watch the enormous stream gushing out and exclaim 'Look! All you have to do is turn that thing and you have all the water you want!'

When it was time to leave, Lawrence found these men trying to remove the faucets. Astounded, he asked them what they were doing. 'We will take these back to the desert and then we will never lack for water.' So Lawrence had to explain that the faucets had to be attached to a source of water.

People oftentimes do just the same thing. They try to get a flow from faucets that are not attached. Our faucets are all the little forms of faith and tradition: praying regularly and all the rest.

GET STRONG

$\mathcal{N}$obody can live successfully in this world without being strong. You may be pampered and protected when you are a child, but you have to learn to be strong as you mature, because sooner or later, life will throw the book at you. Sometimes it will throw the whole book at you all at once. You have to get adjusted so you won't collapse under the trouble, or give way under difficulty, or fold under the blow of adversity. I sometimes think that the greatest virtue of all is to be strong.

Religion is a way of life that makes people strong. You can have all the strength you will ever need if you build into yourself the love of God and stay close to Him until He becomes part of you.

ENJOY THE WORLD

$\mathcal{T}$he world is a wonderful place. We were put into it by a God who loved us and wanted to surround us with that which would develop us, so that ultimately He could take us out of this world of the temporal into the world of the eternal.

Certain theological circles have put forth the notion that too much enjoyment of the physical world is pantheistic, even pagan, but I reject this attitude completely. I believe that the hills, the seas, the stars, the sky, the sun, the rain, and the snow reflect a greater spiritual world. The purpose of material forms is only to give substance and reality to the world of the spirit. The person who associates with the natural world, thinking of it spiritually, will find his spirit refreshed, his mind cleansed; he will be stimulated and inspired.

DYNAMIC ENGRAVINGS

*H*ope and expectation are two dynamic words that can change your life. Write these words in gigantic letters across the sky of your life, as you sometimes see skywriting advertisements against the heavens. Deeply embed these until they become a motivational part of your whole being.

Do this and your life will be good, very good, no matter how much pain or difficulty you experience.

THE PLANTED INSTINCT

$\mathcal{I}$ remember sitting on the porch with my mother and saying, 'Mother, I want to amount to something. I'm going to make money and come back with enough to buy and sell some of these people around here.'

But my mother said, 'Ambition, Norman, is good if God controls it. But what I want you to be is a clean, decent, honourable, upright man with love in your heart, serving God and His children; and I want you to live so that when you finish your course of life, I'll meet you somewhere in the eternities of our Lord.'

That sounds sentimental. But this is the ideal that mothers have put into us — or rather that they have in us the instinct to be children of God. So touch the hem of His garment that you may be made perfectly whole.

EXPECT A MIRACLE

A man told me about a business associate who once enclosed a card in one of his letters. On one side, the card said, 'Expect a miracle.' And on the other, 'God is on your side.' The man was about to throw it out, but the card intrigued him. He put it in his wallet.

Every time he opened his wallet, this card would fall out: 'Expect a miracle.' 'God is on your side.' The message began to seep into his consciousness. He began to send up little prayers. Then he started adopting a positive attitude toward the problems that had baffled and frustrated and defeated him. And finally, he began expecting a miracle.

You get what you expect. Life is full of all kinds of disappointments and sorrows, but it is also full of wonders. And if you expect wonderful things, wonderful things will happen. When God is on your side, you can expect a miracle.

AN 'INNER EAR'

𝒯he Lord does speak to people. And there is such a thing as an inner ear with which you hear His voice. Where you really hear is deep in your soul. Stanley Jones heard. The Lord said to him, 'I want you to do a job for Me in India. You can't do it the way you are, breaking down all the time. Will you give Me your worries, your anxieties? If you will. I'll give you such health as you never dreamed of.'

'Lord' said Jones, 'I'll close that bargain right away.' I heard Dr. Jones say twenty years after this event, 'Since that night I never had another breakdown. I had not only physical health, but I had mental and spiritual health as well. I seemed to have tapped new life for body, mind, and spirit. And I had done nothing but take it!'

I tell you, friends, what can be done for a human being seems so incredible that the person who hasn't the eye or the ear of faith can hardly understand it. So let God help you. He will help you and He will do it soon.

ENJOY LIFE

$\mathscr{I}$ have always maintained that it is an objective of God that people shall live happy lives. Of course, the word *happiness* is sometimes used in a very superficial sense. Maybe the word *joy* is better, for it suggests something deeper.

I realize that the minute I make that statement, I am bound to be criticized by the small, supercilious, sophisticated group of articulate preachers who seem to think that nobody should be happy. I don't know what they want for humanity unless they want everybody to be miserable. In some circles there seems to be a notion that a person cannot be a true Christian unless he goes around with a sour look on his face. This is a distortion. It is a carry-over of a mistaken notion that it is a sin to enjoy life.

WE NEED TURBULENCE!

One day I was on a Boeing 707, and the pilot came back and sat down beside me for a few minutes. I happened to look out the window and saw something I didn't understand. I said, 'Captain, out there along the wing, there are blades set at intervals. What are those things?'

'Those are vortex generators,' he replied. 'When we have a smooth flow of air, these big planes don't steer as perfectly as they do when there is slight turbulence. The flow of air swirling around those blades gives us enough turbulence for perfect performance.'

If you had nothing but absolutely smooth flight conditions on the voyage of life, you wouldn't attain the objective for which you are designed. So the Lord has put vortex generators into human existence in order that we may grow strong and learn to steer our course and arrive at the destination He has set for us. These vortex generators seem very big sometimes, and we feel defeated by them. But a person is lifted above defeat by getting hold of the hope we have in God.

THE FORCE THAT MAKES
THE DIFFERENCE

*W*e all have problems and difficulties, and sometimes these seem overwhelming. But the Bible says, 'If God is for us, who can be against us?' No matter what problems or difficulties you may have, you can conquer them and, not only that, you can be more than a conqueror.

How can one overcome failure that comes from negative attitudes? One way, and a very important one, is to practice seeing everything as developing rather than as deteriorating. See only good coming to you. Practice visualizing it. Practice being conscious for it. Really see it coming to you and practice thanking God for it. There is a law whereby in so doing, you actually attract it to yourself.

BETTER WAYS TO
BETTER DAYS

$\mathcal{T}$he Bible like other holy books is a straightforward, honest book. It does not guarantee freedom from pain, sorrow, trouble, difficulty, or heartache, but it does promise inner happiness and good days. So to have better ways to better days, keep all this in the background of your mind.

One way to realize better days is to live honestly. How many people live with absolute honesty? Have you ever been completely honest with yourself? Have you ever told yourself the whole truth about yourself? Have you ever faced yourself, not as you think you are, but as you really are? How long has it been since you made an appraisal of your strengths and your weaknesses? Do you know whether you are deteriorating or growing? Are you a better, more confident, more knowledgeable person now than you were ten years ago — or are you a worse person now than you were ten years ago? Honesty is the first principle for having better ways to better days.

YOU ARE A CHILD OF GOD

*F*aith is an acceptance of spiritual truth, a belief in yourself as a child of God. I think everybody, once every day, ought to draw himself up and say, 'I am a child of God.' And when you believe that, you begin to release powers within your mind, your soul, that can lift you above your defeats. If you just stay at your earthly level, then when you look up at these great big defeating problems, they will overwhelm you.

But as a child of God, you are much taller than you are on your own. You have an extension, by the power of faith, you can overcome any difficulty in this world. The problems of life are infinitesimal in comparison with the extension powers that are in you as a child of God. You may have problems; they may seem very big to you. But you yourself are much bigger than you think. I've seen it happen again and again: God comes into a man's mind, into his thought; and the inspiration produces an explosion, and the man rises above his difficulty.

THE RELIGION OF LOVE

*P*eople practice different kinds of religion. They observe a formal kind, which means carrying out precepts and following the proper forms. They practice a doctrinal religion, which is acknowledging certain truths and creeds. Unfortunately, that is as far as most people ever get.

But there are those who find a lifesaving, life-changing religon. They come upon a power, and it helps them to overcome pain, weakness, sorrow, frustrations, and defeats. It gives them a sparkle in their eyes, a glow on their face, and an elasticity in their step. It changes them so that they love everybody. Their whole life flows out to bless humankind.

LIVE IN ABUNDANCE

$\mathscr{D}$o you know the meaning of the word *abundance?* I didn't, until I looked it up one time. And I was thrilled. The derivation of the word goes back to the Latin verb *undare*, which means 'to rise up in waves.' Isn't that great? Life rises up in waves. Have you got any waves of life? Or are you living on little dribbles? Almighty God is a generous God. He never meant that we should dribble through life. He intended us to live in abundance.

Of all handicaps that hold people back from being successful in their living, from overcoming weakness and having strength, the worst is a lack of love. There is no wisdom like that of the scriptures, which tells us not to be angry with people and not to hate them, but to love them; not to be irritable with people, but to love and serve them. If you so live, life will flow back to you in great waves.

WHEN FACED WITH DIFFICULTIES...

$\mathcal{T}$rue optimism is the belief that the good of life outweights the evil, and there is always an inherent good behind a difficulty. When faced with difficulties, the optimist does not say, 'Isn't this awful?' but says to the Lord, 'Lord, You've given me a difficulty, but I know there must be good in it, and I will seek to find that good.'

Most people underestimate themselves. And if you underestimate yourself, you will be underestimated by others. Your achievements in life agree with your own appraisal of your capacities.

RELEASED FROM A PRISON

A mixed-up, defeated man started coming to Marble Collegiate Church; one day he found Someone here, that Someone who can change any individual. This is a letter that he wrote me:

Dear Dr. Peale,
As you well know, alcohol was not the only problem I had six years ago. I was one of the most negative people anybody ever met. I was one of the most super-critical, impatient, cocky individuals that you could imagine. Now, please don't think that I have overcome all these things. I haven't. At times I become discouraged with my progress. Gradually, by trying to follow the teachings of Jesus, I am learning to control myself and be less critical. It is like being released from a prison. I never dreamed life could be so wonderful.

Do as this man did and you will say to yourself with gladness in your heart, 'How good God is.'

EVERYONE NEEDS
A NEW HEART

A friend of mine has always impressed me with his vivacity, his sense of delight in life, his eagerness. I asked him once how he managed this, and he said, 'I pass expectancy thoughts through my mind every morning.' What a technique!

Another vibrant friend explains his secret for living joyously and without boredom this way: 'Every morning I read the Bible, spend ten minutes in quiet meditation, and close by saying. "O Lord, thank You so much for the eventful day You are going to give me." And I do have one eventful day after another, days filled with joy and excitement.'

How is your heart? Everyone needs a new heart at times, for the old one gets tired. How is your spirit? Everyone needs a new spirit at times, for the old spirit often becomes weary. If you haven't got a joyous heart and spirit, let God give it to you.

LIVE WITH DELIGHT

$\mathcal{H}$ow much of religion do you want? Are you content to have merely a set of ethics? Or would you like to be deeply stirred and released? James Russell Lowell in his poem, *The Cathedral*, wrote:

> I, that still pray at morning and at eve…
>> Thrice in my life perhaps have truly prayed.
> Thrice, stirred below my conscious self, have felt
>> That perfect disenthrallment which is God.

There is a power that can lift us above ourselves; give us victory over all our weaknesses; fill our minds with courage and make us count in the day and age in which we live; make us flaming tongues of fire to live with power. And only a few people reach for it. The others are content with something halfway alive. But a human being is meant to be a tremendous person.

One way to start becoming such a person is to say, 'By the grace and power of God, I'm going to find interest in life. I'm going to put interest into my living. I'm going to live with delight. I'm going to live with enthusiasm.'

HOW ARE YOU TODAY?

𝒜rriving by train to speak at a rally in Pennsylvania, I headed for a cab. A sombre man was sitting in the front seat with the driver, and a woman was in one corner of the back seat. I got in and took the other corner. Then along came another woman with a suitcase and a couple of paper bags. I moved over and she got in. Then she took us all into her love. She asked, 'How are you all today?' I said I felt fine.

The man in front turned around and asked. 'What makes you so happy?'

'God makes me happy,' the woman replied. 'I used to be the most miserable woman in Pennsylvania. But I found God.' And by the time she got out, she had made us all happy.

LET GOD BE IN CHARGE

A few years ago, a Rotarian came to the New York club labouring under terrible sorrow. His son Steve had fallen into trouble; he had driven a stolen car over several state lines and was in jail in New York. The father had come to the Rotary Club for comfort and assistance.

The club turned the problem over to two laymen. They got in touch with me and explained that they'd been appointed as a committee to handle this case and asked if I would help. They said, 'We want Jesus Christ on this committee, too, because only He can help this father and this boy.' Later they came to my study and we prayed together, putting Steve and his father in the hands of God. And He took charge.

We went to the judge in the case and the boy was paroled to us. A few years later, Steve became a pastor. Moreover, his seminary sent him to other seminaries to testify to the students what can happen to an individual who meets God.

IT HAPPENS FOR THE BEST

*M*y friend Richard Prentice Ettinger, who founded the Prentice-Hall publishing company, was present at a breakfast I attended. He'd had throat cancer and had a little tube in his throat, but he spoke distinctly and well.

That morning we had a wonderful conversation. In the course of it he said, 'You know my theory that whatever happens, happens for the best? When I got cancer I thought, "Oh, oh! How is this going to be for the best?" The cancer took twenty pounds off me. The doctors said afterward that the weight had been affecting my heart. Because the excess weight is gone, I will live ten years longer. Whatever happens, happens for the best.

One of the greatest things that ever happened for the best in my life was to know an undefeatable man like Richard Prentice Ettinger, who demonstrated in the most difficult circumstances that if you do your best and you put it in the hands of God, you can make things happen for the best.

ELEMENT OF SILENCE

Quietness is a profoundly creative element. Who was the tallest character who ever rose up from among the American people? Well, in my book, it was Abraham Lincoln.

Now Lincoln in his early years was fortunate enough to live in the virgin forests of the Middle West. As a distinguished writer on Lincoln once observed, 'In the making of him, the element of silence was immense.' Great trees that seemed to scrape the sky were his companions, the silence of the forest whispered its wisdom to him, and later, in the days of crisis, he was sustained because he had within him quietness, from which he drew confidence.

We're too noisy; we're too hectic. We're too disturbed; we're too confused. We have noise all the time. Consequently, we have noise inside. So we lose our confidence. Then we lose our strength. Remember: 'I will make you strong if you quietly trust me.'

THE TWO PILLARS

$\mathcal{S}$ir Arnold Lunn was an authority on the geography of Switzerland. He travelled over practically every valley, every mountain and wrote about them with the fervour of a poet. In the summer of 1940, when the German army was marching into France, Lunn was summoned to England. At Berne he looked at the mountains and wondered whether he would be back.

The war ceased. Lunn arrived at Berne in the late afternoon. The sky was overcast, the mountains invisible. Suddenly the clouds parted, and there they stood. The light of the sun upon them seemed to say that there are certain things in life which no cloud, no war, no hate, no force can destroy. This was for Arnold Lunn a spiritual experience, reassuring him that no matter how much suffering exists, God remains.

So I would say that there are two pillars upon which happiness rests. One is moral decency, mastery over self. The other is the knowledge of the love of God and of His presence at all times, come what may.

THE SECRET THAT TOLSTOY LEARNT

Leo Tolstoy went through his whole calendar of sins trying to make life good. But it was dust and ashes. He knew he had to find the secret of life. He went out into the country where he met peasants and said to them, 'My friends, you must teach me your secret.'

They said, 'When you stay in contact with God, joy is continuous. But if you get away from God, you get away from the life force. Return to God and you will find good days.'

Tolstoy wrestled with himself, because there were some things he didn't want to let go. Then one day he gave it all up; he accepted God and gave himself to Him. He wrote later that he had no sooner done this than joyous waves of life seemed to surge through him.

You can make your days good. But in the deeper sense of the word, they are made good by God. I like that picture of Tolstoy — joyous waves of life surging in and out of him.

THE HELMET OF HOPE

*A*n analysis was made of the experiences of two thousand American soldiers in World War II who were taken prisoner by the Nazis. All had been in concentration camps where they were brainwashed, beaten, starved, and treated wih indignity. Many died; others became physical wrecks; others were emotionally maimed.

But a small group of men emerged unhurt mentally, spiritually, or physically. These men had decided that they wouldn't let the terrible circumstances destroy them. They kept their spirits up by telling one another about how wonderful life was going to be when they got back to the United States. They described the girls they were going to marry and their plans for the futures of their children. In other words, they practiced hope. And they were saved by hope. Hope is one of the great blessings offered to us by Jesus Christ. Put on the helmet of hope and change your thought processes.

FINDING GOOD DAYS

$\mathcal{S}$o how do you find good days? It is very simple. If you want to be happy, if you want to have good days, just skip the evil and go for the good. It is just that open and shut.

Sit down with yourself and ask, what is my worst weakness? Don't ask your spouse what your chief weakness is. He or she will probably name a half dozen. Just ask yourself, 'What is my chief fault?'

When you find it, study it. Maybe it is the thing that has been holding you back from better days. Once having isolated it, once having faced it honestly, you can decide what you are going to do about it, with the help of the God. A person who is honest with himself, who has isolated his faults and taken them to God, can do something about them. And when a real fault is out of your way, what glorious, better days you can have!

THE JUNGFRAU

*W*hile I was vacationing in Switzerland, a troubled young man visited me. We went to a little café in Interlaken. There is a meadow in the heart of the town, and towering over this meadow is the great mountain, the Jungfrau (Young Wife). Like a coy young wife, she often throws a veil of clouds over her face. That morning, however, the veil had been cast aside and there she was, in all of her white, sparkling, radiant glory. We sat at the café. The boy gazed at the mountain and said, 'That's the way I want to be: clean, like that!'

'You can be,' I said, 'if you will bring Jesus Christ into your life.'

'Oh,' he exclaimed, 'thank God! That's what I wanted to hear you say!' Apparently nobody else had said that to him. He leaned over the table where we were having coffee and at my urging gave his heart to Jesus Christ.

'Go up there among the mountains where it is clean and talk with God,' I said. That boy now knows that not only is there real good in life, but he knows where to find it.

NEVER GIVE UP

*I*f you have no confidence; if you're defeated; if you're being beaten down; if you're troubled by fear, diffidence, apprehension, or weakness; then come to where the power is, where the confidence is to be found: in your faith, in the Saviour.

It is good that we should call Him Saviour, because that is what He does. He saves you from your defeats and gives you confidence with which you can handle life with mastery, satisfaction, and happiness. You can have confidence. You must have confidence if you are going to live well. Never let anything get you down — no matter how difficult, how black, how hard it is, no matter how hopeless it may seem or how utterly depressed you may become. Whatever the quality and the character of the circumstances involved, never let anything get you down. Always, there is help and hope for you.

WALK AROUND IT

*W*hen faced with a difficult problem — whether it be a health problem, or a domestic problem — walk around it prayerfully.

Now that phrase is not my own — I only wish it were. It was given to me by one of the greatest persons I ever knew. He used to say, 'Let's lay the problem out there on the table, boys, and walk around it prayerfully.' And he would tell us threre is no problem in this world that doesn't have a soft spot somewhere. 'Walk around it prayerfully,' he would say. 'Poke at it until you find the soft spot.'

'Well,' you say, 'that may be all right, but you don't know my problem. My problem is a hard one.' I know. Sure, your problem is a hard one. Just walk around it a little more — prayerfully — and you'll get your answer.

CLOUDED MINDS.
CLEAR MINDS

*K*nowing yourself and getting yourself healed can be a long, hard process if you try to do it by yourself. But the mysterious power of God is such that He comes into the life of anyone who will permit Him to do so and transforms it utterly, releasing the person.

As we go along through life, our minds get clouded so that they do not function in a clear, clean-cut manner anymore. Nervous apprehension or ill will, sinfulness or vindictiveness creeps in; you take yourself too seriously or you live with yourself too much so that your mind gets confused.

There are behaviours and ways of thought which just are not compatible with real happiness. Most of the frustration in our lives is self-imposed frustration. And God offers us release from it, calling us to know the truth, so that the truth may sweep the dust from our minds and we may be free.

HAVE FAITH ...

*Y*ou want to live a successful, meaningful existence. How much do you want that? Well, the Scriptures tells us that things will happen to us according to our faith.

You may say, 'That's okay; I go for that and I believe it; but it is awfully hard to have that kind of faith.' That's right. It is. Because faith has to be practiced. Some people have a greater capacity to believe than others, and it is part of the job of a therapist or counsellor to help an ill or disturbed person to develop his capacity to believe. When such a person gets to the point where he can truly believe, where he can trust faith, he can get well. Faith will heal.

Faith may seem to be an unsubstantial thing to put your feet down on, and you may be inclined to think that the wise ways of the world are better. But if you learn to have faith in faith and believe in it, it will see you through.

QUITE AN OFFER

A young man I knew wanted to be a social worker, but he did not have enough education to qualify. He worked nights driving a rickety truck. One Sunday he had the radio on. A voice was saying, 'Believe in the potential you possess, and yield to the One who has the infinite skills to bring your potential into action.'

He wan't too impressed, but he took to listening to that programme every week. Finally one night he said, 'Okay, Lord, if this is true, please help me.' He described his goal and said, 'I can't do it without You.'

Soon he began to work days and went to school at night. Not long ago, he wrote a letter telling me: 'I am now a social worker, and I am having the time of my life helping people. I will never quit. I will believe.'

Now what do you call that? A miracle of real faith! God doesn't say you have to have a lot of faith, just a little real faith. Quite an offer, isn't it?

THE GREATEST TRUTH

$\mathcal{M}$y wife taught me one of the greatest truths in the world: God is always with you. And I can guarantee to you what she guaranteed to me: if you put your problems in His hands and trust Him, He will guide you and bless you and take care of you till the day you die. And He won't stop there. He will take care of you the rest of the way.

'Well,' you may say, 'that is sensible; that is logical, but I never felt any closeness to God.' I'm sorry to hear anyone say that. Are you going to live all your life and never feel the presence of God? Haven't you had some high moments spiritually, when you felt lifted out of yourself, lifted to a higher level? At some time in your life, you should feel deeply the presence of God. Then, even though there be times when you feel that He is far away from you; you know He is with you, and then nothing can overcome you.

LIVING UNDER PRESSURE

*O*ne part of learning to live successfully under pressure is to analyse our lives and honestly face any of our attitudes that would be a cause of pressure. What most often breaks people down is an impairment of the mental processes by negative thoughts and feelings, or the weight of sin upon their souls. Fear, hate, and resentment give rise to tensions that become continuous, preventing adequate relaxation between peaks of activity. Eventually they so impair a person's resiliency that the daily pressures get him down.

If you are so fortunate as never to have had a crisis, you can count on one thing — you will have a crisis sooner or later. And it will take all your faith, all your strength, all your thought, everything you've got, to meet it. But remember that in any crisis, you have a big God you can turn to in order to find the answer that answers.

NEVER LET ANYTHING
GET YOU DOWN

*M*ary B. Crowe rose from humble circumstances to become one of the most successful insurance agents in the United States. At the age of twelve, Mary was left in charge at home. She got the meals for a family of ten, cleaned the house, did the laundry, and went to school.

Later, after she became the first college graduate in the history of her family, she decided she wanted to be a life insurance agent. At that time, the idea of women selling life insurance was practically unheard of. She asked to see a manager about selling insurance, and he did his best to discourage her. Long after he had retired, that agency manager was present at a luncheon in honour of Mary B. Crowe's twenty-fifth anniversary.

If you remember God's everlasting presence and look to Him for help, nothing will be so hard that you cannot think it through and see it through. So you need never let anything ever get you down, you wonderful person.

WHEN CLOUDS GATHER

After a speaking engagement in Florida, my hosts assigned a Navy captain to fly me home. En route, the captain told me that there was a very heavy overcast in New York. 'As a matter of fact,' he said, 'we'll have to go in on instruments.' We went down, down, down. And finally, I saw the lights of the runway and we came right up to the ramp. It was a beautiful landing.

The captain said, 'The primary ingredient for a good landing is faith. I have to have faith in these instruments. If I didn't, I might think, "Well, maybe this instrument isn't exactly right, so I'll make this adjustment." And that could have tragic consequences.'

Your religious education is your instrument panel for safe navigation through the long flight of the years. When clouds gather, storms develop, and trouble looms, if you lose faith in your instruments, you can be lost. But if you have faith in the teachings of the Scriptures, in prayer, in goodness, love, and hope, your instruments will bring you through.

MY PHILOSOPHY
AND MY FAITH

𝓜y friend built a house in Topanga Canyon — a beautiful place in an attractive, wild setting. I was in Los Angeles when a fire swept through the canyon and destroyed 565 houses. My friend's house was among the ruined buildings. I telephoned and said, 'I'm sorry that your house burned down.'

'Why, what are you worrying about me for?' he said. 'Sure it burned. But my wife and kids are safe.'

'Did you save anything from the house?' I asked.

'Nothing but my philosophy and my faith,' he said, 'But that's all I need. I'm going to build again. Don't worry about me until I get into some real trouble.'

That is the kind of talk I like to hear: Nothing left but 'my philosophy and my faith!' If you'll start digging into your religious faith and applying its principles, you will be able to meet and handle victoriously the tough situations of life.

PACK MEANING WITH YOUR LIFE!

A young man was sitting next to me on a plane. It was so dark that the lights had to be turned on. But we took off with clockwork precision, and in seconds we were above the overcast and into the clear afternoon sky.

I was in the window seat. Suddenly I felt a boy leaning over to see this marvellous sight. He exclaimed, 'Did you ever see anything like it? To come out of darkness into this glorious light — isn't it something? Don't tell me God isn't in His heaven!'

I looked at the young man's face. It was the great, full face of someone who loved life and loved the world. And he poured out to me his hopes, his dreams, his ideals and objectives. All of them had to do with human justice and making the world a better place. He had meaning packed into his life.

There are people everywhere who pack meaning into their lives because they pack something else into their lives: faith and goodness and love and hope and fellowship, and every other good thing.

WORD OF GOD

$\mathcal{I}$ once met a man known as Brother Andrew. Hearing that people in Communist lands wanted the Word of God, he went to the missionary society in Amsterdam and asked them to send him to Eastern Europe. They said, 'No, it's too dangerous.'

'Will you pray for me if I go on my own?' he asked. He fixed up a car so it could conceal a supply of Bibles, and he crossed the border with them. Finally he was caught. But the border agents knew how valuable the Bibles were; they confiscated them and sold them for high prices. This didn't bother Brother Andrew, because at least his Bibles were getting into circulation. He returned to that border seven more times to get the agents to sell more Bibles.

Sitting and talking with this dedicated man, I asked him. 'Why do you do this?'

He looked at me and answered, 'I do it because the only thing that can set these people free is the Word of God.'

ANTIDOTE OF FEAR

$\mathcal{W}$e are either destroyed or made whole by the kind of thoughts we think. You can cancel out a fearful thought or an apprehensive thought with a faith thought. Don't be afraid — just believe. If you have been victimized by the fear of some sinister thing that might happen down the road, just believe and healing will start. If you believe strongly enough, you can drive any apprehensive fear out of your mind. So the number one antidote for fear is to fill your mind full of God.

This may seem to you to be a strange expression. How can you get your mind full of God? Well, you read about God, you think about God, you talk to God, you try to serve God, you try to live God's way. After a while your mind gets full of God. And when your mind is full of God, it cannot have anything negative in it. It can't have prejudice; it can't have hate; it can't have resentment; it can't have impurities of any kind. It becomes wholesome and good.

THE TREMENDOUS PRINCIPLE

$\mathcal{I}$ was invited to a gathering to honour the mothers who had lost sons in the war. I went with the understanding that I was to give an invocation. But when I picked up the programme I saw that I was on the programe to make a speech! I was aghast. I had no confidence.

General Theodore Roosevelt, Jr. was sitting next to me. He said, 'Each of those mothers has lost the idol of her heart. Can't you get up and tell them that God loves them and their country loves them and at some time, somewhere, in the mercy of God, they will meet their sons again? Forget about yourself, son. Put yourself in the hands of God and do the best you can.'

To this day I love that man, for he taught me a tremendous principle: love other people, do the best you can, and put your faith in God. These are the secrets of confidence and security in an insecure world.

THE SECRET OF HAPPINESS

*W*hat kind of people are happy people? In reply to this question, some would say that the mood of unhappiness today is very high. A distinguished writer declared in a magazine article that unhappiness is the commonest thing there is. And T.S. Eliot, the famous British poet and literary critic, once asked plaintively, 'Where is the life we have lost in living?'

A great many writers, perhaps because they themselves have lost the secret of happiness, dwell on the prevalence of unhappiness. But I believe there are untold numbers of people who have discovered a precious secret, the secret of how to have happiness in depth. And, as a matter of fact, unless there is depth in happiness, it isn't genuine. It is spurious and of little value. Apparently many people are discovering this. They are finding out how to live in this confused and bewildering world, while at the same time having peace within their hearts and a deep happiness within their natures.

NEVER ACCEPT DEFEAT

It is really unworthy of a person to say, 'Well, I guess I've had it. It's too much for me. I can't handle it anymore. I will just accept defeat.'

You say, 'Look at all the difficulties.' I am looking at them. Our forefathers made a new world. Were our forefathers any greater than we are? We too can make a new world if we think we can and if we have the same quality of faith as they had. No, we don't need to be defeated by anything. Never accept defeat.

If you feel defeated and you think, 'I'm tired and weary and I've had it,' that is exactly how it will be. You can count on it for sure. You will be what you accept in your mind. But if, on the contrary, when the going gets difficult, you think, 'I won't accept this — I will continue to think victory and not defeat,' then what happens is that all the resources of your nature flow toward effecting a victory situation and circumventing a defeat condition.

THE GREATEST THINGS IN
WORLD ARE SIMPLE

$\mathscr{C}$arl Erskine, the great pitcher for the Brooklyn Dodgers, once told me, 'The simplest and greatest truth that I have ever learned in my whole life is this: Whatever the problem, whatever the challenge, difficulty, hardship, pain, or suffering — you need never have confidence knocked out of your heart if you believe and remember that God is with you, and if you submit your life into His hands.'

I know this sounds simple. The greatest things in this world are simple. Religion does not mean complexity. It takes the complex and inscrutable and makes it so simple that a child can understand. Just put your life in God's hands; do the best you can, trust it to Him, and you will have the blessing of confidence. It does not come easily. It requires practice. But when you get it, then you have the secret of peace and confidence.

BRING IN THE MIGHTY SHOULDERS

A company was building a bridge and discovered a sunken ship in the channel where they had to put down some footings. They had to get it out of the way. A young crewman suggested a solution. He said to the foreman, 'Sir, if I were you, I would send down a diver to work chains underneath the hulk and attach the chains to flat boats on either side. Let the tide float it out.'

The foreman saw the reasonableness in the suggestion and adopted it, and presently the ocean tide came surging into the harbour. The shoulders of the sea got under those flat boats and lifted the hulk free.

Now haven't you seen people wearing themselves out, trying to lift a great weight, when through surrender to God, they could get the mighty shoulders of God under it? Let God help you. The power of God will flow to your aid if you give yourself to Him, commit yourself to Him, and have faith in Him.

OUR CIVILIZATION CAN DECAY

𝒯he problem of preserving our country is acute. We do not realize how easily a civilization can decay. I have been to Byblos, at the eastern end of the Mediterranean Sea, where you can see at a glance the excavated traces of seven successive civilizations (thanks to the skill with which the excavations there have been performed): Egyptian, Persian, Greek, Roman, and others — all mighty civilizations.

If at the height of any of those civilizations, a preacher had stood in a pulpit and said, 'This civilization can die,' he would have been laughed at. But they all did die, and their cities were covered over by dirt and sand and a few crumbling monuments. That is all that is left of them. This mighty civilization of ours likewise has within it the seeds of death. All human beings have within them the seeds of death. You have them; I have them. It is necessary to counteract these seeds of death with those of life. Our civilization can die, or our civilization can live.

DELIVER POWER

Of people will love the dear Lord and love others and love this beautiful world they will overcome fear. A great factor in overcoming fear is in getting a sound mind. Think of all the tangled ideas to which we have been subjected and from which we may never have escaped — quirks, notions, ghosts, shadows in the mind — affecting our attitudes toward ourselves and toward the world. A sound, clean, wholesome mind is a mental machine in which there is no sand — finely lubricated and working with precision.

When you have a mind like that, you have a mental engine that delivers power. Difficulties start with obsessive things that you pick up over the years: prejudices, hates, notions, fears, tensions, opinions of yourself that are incorrect. When you begin to know God, when you learn to love Him, then you begin to see yourself as you really are, not as you had thought you were, you cast out defeatist elements.

CHANGED THINKING

A popular local television host invited me to his studio for an interview. When I met him, I was rather startled. He was abnormally short, and his hands were disproportionately large with stubby fingers. He had an unimaginative face, but when he began to talk, his countenance became animated; his eyes flashed with depths of understanding. There was a tremendous charm about the man.

Before we went on the air he told me, 'I was a defeated person. I was self-conscious and resentful. I think you can understand why: you have only to look at me. However, some instinct kept telling me that being bitter would only make things worse. In my unhappiness I began to read the Bible. Gradually a big idea dawned upon me: changed thinking changes everything. So I resolved that I would learn to think spiritually about my handicap. And as I did so, everything changed for me.'

I knew why his show was so popular. Even when he talked about ordinary things, he gave people something special.

HAVE YOU EVER USED
ALL YOUR STRENGTH

$\mathcal{J}$ust what does the process of praying do for you to relieve you of worry? One thing it does is release and activate your built-in strength. Every one of us has more strength by far than he ever dreamed of. Have you ever used all your strength? *All* of it? No, you have never used one-half of your strength, nor have I. I'll go further and say that I doubt that any of us has ever used one-tenth of his strength.

We have tremendous reservoirs of power that we could call into action if we wanted to. The greatest achievement in life is to know how to continually break out from yourself the strength that is there. You pray the strength out, you believe it out, you practice it out. And then the worry fades away. It is amazing the strength that people have — that you have, that I have.

If power isn't coming through, find the block and remove it. Always poke around a problem, looking for its soft spot, for nearly every problem has one. Then break the problem open and find the solution.

PRACTICE HAPPINESS

$\mathcal{I}$ had a friend who managed a hotel in Florida who was one of the happiest men I ever saw. He had a very interesting way of starting the day. The first thing he did in the morning was go down to the ocean and take a dip. No matter what the weather was, he did this every morning. And just before plunging in he would offer this prayer: 'O God, as I breathe into me this fresh morning air, so I breathe in Your Holy Spirit. Come fill me with Your holiness, fill me with Your peace, fill me with Your kindness, Your purity and wisdom. Fill me with Your joy. And O God, fill me with Yourself.'

Then he would plunge into the sea and come out feeling alive to his fingertips, a song on his lips, vital and vibrant for the day. That was how he began his daily practice of happiness. And his joyous personality was impressive evidence that by practice we can be happy people, notwithstanding difficulties and adversities. So don't continue practicing old unhappiness. Practice happiness.

DON'T LOSE YOUR DREAMS

*W*hat is the highest form of God's creation? Human nature — with its weaknesses, but with its strength; with its defeat, but with its victory; with its sins, but with its goodness; with its unlimited possibility under God? What, then, would you like to be? You name it, and by God's grace, you can be it.

You may say, 'That is going too far. That is promising too much.' But I have not said you can attain this through your own strength, because you cannot. You are weak. You are of the world, earthy. But you are also of heaven, heavenly. And through God's grace, you can realize your highest dreams.

As a child, you had long, long thoughts of what you might become. Have you now become so old and tired and cynical that you have forgotten these dreams of your youth, these high expectations of yourself? Never lose them, no matter what else you lose. Lose your stock certificates, lose your property; but don't lose your dreams. For this urge to be someone, to be something, was put into you by Almighty God.

I HAVE NEWS FOR YOU

*O*f you are discouraged, I have news for you — good news.

There is a way to end discouragement. And the word itself gives the clue. *Discouragement* is formed by putting the prefix *dis-* before the word courage. In effect, you have a discounting of courage. Therefore, the way to end discouragement is to remove the prefix and to lay under your life a solid foundation of courage.

Winston Churchill expresses it well. He says, 'Success is never final. Failure is never fatal. It's courage that counts.'

WALK AWAY FROM YOUR YESTERDAYS

*S*ome people must be revised in order that they may have a new life every morning. If you become a revised, new person, your tomorrows will be altogether different. I'd like to relate to you a letter that illustrates this point. It is from a woman who lives in Columbia, Missouri. She says: 'I never before knew the effective use of faith. Now I find myself practicing my beliefs and, as a result, I have a cheerful outlook. I have been able to make new friends out of old enemies. I finally learned and accepted the fact that no one was against me but myself. I have come out of my shell at long last. I cannot adequately describe the happiness I now feel, instead of the self-pity and self-hate that once was me.'

This woman walked away from her yesterdays. She applied the principle that by personal revision with God's help, you can become a new person. It is a simple formula. It takes discipline, it takes effort; but you can work it if you really want it, and thus be able to start life new every morning.

DO YOU BELIEVE?

$\mathcal{B}$elief is the key to a transformed life. Hear the words of the Gospel of Luke, 'Give, and it will be given to you.' Now the question is: Do we believe that? Do you believe that if you do so it will work?

The first thing is to believe in faith and trust it. The second thing is to go out and practice faith. Actually, there isn't much of a distinction between believing in faith and practicing it, because if you truly do believe, you practice it. For the person who learns the techniques of faith and practices them, nothing is too good to be true. If you are sick, you believe that God with the doctor will heal you; if you are weak, you believe you will become strong; if you have a great opportunity, you believe that you can handle it. You trust and you do the best you can. Whatever the situation is, you believe in and practice faith.

THE AMAZING TRUTH

*Y*ou can find amazing truth all caught up in one verse from the Bible: 'The fear of the Lord is the beginning of wisdom, and knowledge of the Holy One is understanding.' Any person who needs a change within himself or within his life can have this take place by changing his mind. But this cannot be a superficial mental change; it must be one in depth. Such a change can be extremely effective.

Are you perhaps facing a hard situation? Are you involved in some unsatisfactory personal relationship? Is there some other kind of trouble in your life? We could hardly enumerate all the problems a human being has to deal with. But there is a great answer to them all — and it is this: they can all be changed, and you can be changed — everything for the better — through the magic of a positive mental attitude.

GOD SAVED MY BOY

*O*ne day after a speech I gave in Chicago, a young woman in a waitress's uniform rushed up to me and told me her amazing story.

'I have a little boy. When he was five years old, he got sick. The doctor prepared me for the worst. I felt my whole world would go to pieces if I lost my boy. Then a neighbour gave me one of your sermons to read. And in that sermon you said, "If you have a loved one who is ill or about whom you are worried, give the loved one to God." So I prayed and I put my boy in God's hands. And He let me keep my boy. And now God and I are raising him together.'

And so when we separated, I went my way refreshed by yet another wonderful drama of human life rising to high places even out of humble circumstances.

'THOUGHT BURNING'

A church in the southern USA periodically holds what they call a 'thought-burning' service. They bring urns before the altar and light fires in them. Each person in the congregation is given paper on which he is to write the thoughts he wants to be rid of — then, one by one, the congregants file down the aisle, drop their thoughts into the urn, and watch them curl up into ashes.

Well, you don't need an urn to burn your regrets and hates and failures. You can set fire to them in your mind through the cleansing power of the God. Forget past failures. When you have failed, ask God to show you how to do the thing better the next time, and then go back at it and give it all you've got.

THE MIND DETERMINES

$\mathcal{L}$ook at a tough situation this way: 'Well, it does present difficulties. I'm not going to be flippant about it. I know I have a problem here. But God is with me. I have a few friends. And God is helping me. Other people have solved problems like this. So I'm going to pour what confidence I've got right on this difficulty.'

I hope those who read this meditation will start thinking about God, who gives abundantly above what we ask or even think. This is a big promise, isn't it?

He gives us abundance, according to what we ask, more than we ask, above what we can ask, and more than we can even think. That is what He wants to give us all. But whether we receive or take it depends on the power that is working within us. The essence of the matter is the way we think. What goes on in the mind determines everything.

ANOTHER GREAT DAY

*O*nce when I was sitting in a hotel coffee shop having an early breakfast alone, a man came in. With a cheerful good morning to the cashier at the door and to the waiters, he came walking through the place, saw me, and apparently knew me, for he pulled up a chair, asking, 'May I sit with you?' Before I could say yes or no, there he was. He shook out his napkin and exclaimed, 'Boy, this is going to be another great day!'

I was astonished to hear this kind of conversation so early in the morning. 'I gather you've had many good days,' I said.

'Oh, yes,' he assured me. 'I learned that if I pass a series of expectancy thoughts through my mind every morning, God will bring my great expectations to pass. He can bring the good out. Therefore I just go along with Him, passing expectancy thoughts through my mind.'

May I ask you, my reader, a question? What kind of expectancy thoughts have you in your mind right now?

THE RIGHT PRESCRIPTION

$\mathcal{S}$ome time ago, I met with a group of doctors and one of them asked me, 'How many times a year do you discuss the problem of stress and tension from the pulpit?'

'About once a year,' I replied.

He pulled a prescription pad from his pocket, wrote something on it, and pushed it across the table to me. 'This is a prescription I give to patients after I have done everything I can do for them medically.'

On the pad he had written: 'Let God change the way you think.' And lest you think this particular physician is odd, I assure you that his professional standing is extremely high.

I believe that the Bible has the answer to every personal and social problem. And I believe that by using such a great treatment as 'Let God change the way you think.' you can cure yourself of being victimized by pressure.

NOT HOW OLD YOU ARE

𝒯he more you give, the more you shall receive. I saw an example of this at a luncheon for businessmen. The speakers were mostly in their forties, I would say, except for one man who was obviously older than all the rest. I sat down beside him and asked, 'Are you head of one of these businesses here?'

'Sure am,' he answered. 'Why? Don't I look like I could handle it?'

I said, 'I just heard you are eighty years old.'

'Well,' he demanded, 'what's wrong with being eighty years old? It isn't how long you've been around. Don't think that just because I have a game leg, I can't handle the business. You don't run a business with your leg; you run it with your head.'

Naturally, the man had found this zest where it really comes from: through the God, who says He has come that we might have life and have it more abundantly. That is what He offers us. Take it!

CREATIVE SILENCE

$\mathcal{I}$ had a chat with an old friend who had been his state's attorney general. Some years ago, this man said to me, 'If I don't find a way to reduce the tension in my life, I'm going to die.' I discussed the problem with him and advised him to have a quiet time every day for communing with God. Later I saw him and he was quiet, calm, composed, and stronger physically than when he was ten years younger. He told me this was due to the beneficial effect of practicing creative silence.

You are a child of God. God never meant you to be victimized by pressure. He meant you to live in an effective, powerful manner. But that is only possible when you keep Him at the centre of your life and in your own thinking. He will keep you in perfect peace if you keep your mind on Him.

To drop tension from your life, practice getting tranquility by passing peaceful words and thoughts through your mind daily and nightly.

BEETHOVEN'S 'DISASTROUS AFFLICTION'

*W*hen he was thirty-one, Ludwig van Beethoven wrote of the 'disastrous affliction,' the growing deafness, that had befallen him. 'I was soon compelled to keep apart, to live a life of loneliness,' he wrote. 'How could I possibly admit an inferiorty in the one sense that should have been more acute in me than in others? I almost reached the point of putting an end to my life. Only art, it was, that held me back. It seemed impossible to depart this world until I had brought forth all the things I felt inspired to create. And so I went on living this miserable life. O God, You who lookest into the depths of my soul, You understandest me, You knowest that the love of mankind and the desire to do good live with me!'

Beethoven overcame that discouragement. He lived for another twenty-five years, the years of his greatest creativity. Such is the struggle that people have with black moods, and such are the victories of great faith. With the help of God, out of our discouragement and struggle, we may bring messages to bless mankind.

NO TORNADO CAN
SHAKE FAITH

$\mathcal{D}$ r. Robert Schuller grew up in Iowa, and he tells an awe-inspiring story about a tornado. One afternoon Bob and his father heard a rumbling like many freight trains. The sky grew dark. Then out from the dark clouds bulged an enormous funnel.

Seconds later, the whole family was in the car racing down the road. They stopped and watched the tornado hit with elemental force. In ten minutes, it was gone. They saw the whole terrible sight; not one building was still standing — their house had vanished. Mr. Schuller told his wife and young Bob to wait where they were and got out of the car. He went poking in the ruins and brought back a battered motto that had hung in the kitchen. It said, 'Keep looking to Jesus.'

Some people would have lost their faith. But Mr. Schuller rebuilt. He replaced the lost livestock and buildings and equipment. A few years later, farm prices rose sharply. Before long, the mortgage was paid off! He died as the prosperous owner of a thriving farm.

A MAN FROM ELMIRA

A man from Elmira, New York, came to see me in my office. He put his head in his hands and said, 'Everything is lost. It's hopeless.'

'Well,' I said. 'I'd like to explore this. Let me ask you a few questions. Your wife has left you, of course? And no doubt your children are all in jail?'

'What do you mean?' he retorted. 'My wife loves me. Of course she hasn't left me. My kids are good kids. Of course they're not in jail.'

'Well,' I reminded him, 'you told me everything was lost.' We went on through a few more things like that. Then I said, 'Look at the things you've got left! Plus God. Brother, you're in! What do you mean, you want to blow your brains out? All you need to do is blow your faith up.' He found new courage and went home to straighten up his life.

If you are disheartened about anything today, forget it. Blow your faith up. Look to the God. Let Him get into you and change your thinking.

SATISFY YOUR HUNGER

We are given the gift of life. And that is a wonderful thing. But the strange thing is that, having the gift of life, we apparently do not know how to use it. We mess it up. We limit it. We even desecrate it, though it is extraordinarily valuable to us. Many people, no matter how long they may have lived, have never yet grasped the secret of how to handle it. And that is a tragedy.

What, then, is the secret? In the sixth chapter of John's Gospel are these enormous words: 'I am the bread of life.' (That is, 'I put substance into life.') 'He who comes to me will never go hungry.' What a thought! And it goes on to say, 'He who believes in me will never be thirsty.'

Do you ever get hungry? Not the hunger for food, but the hunger for something else, something deep? If you accept Him as the bread of life, you will never be hungry. And what goes for hunger goes for thirst.

BE SOMEONE!

Be someone! What is that supposed to mean? Nowadays everyone wants to be a big shot. What is a big shot? I've heard a big shot defined as a little shot who keeps on shooting. But there are a great many phonies among big shots, as well as a great many fine people.

In any case, to be a big shot or a celebrity is not a goal worthy of a real person. I would say a real person wants to be his or her best self. That is, a real person wants to realize all the potential inside. He or she wants to bring into focus every God-given talent. Such a person wants to attain the best results, not for himself, but for the world and for God. To be someone in that true sense is the highest realization of one's self as a child of God.

We need a reassessment of values. The end of life is to be an organized, integrated, dedicated, useful, outgoing, loving, helpful individual worthy of the approval of God.

THE HIGHEST SECURITY

*O*nce I had the great honour of speaking to the troops in Vietnam. At one place where I was to speak, I noticed a detachment of men on a hilltop about half a mile away. I asked, 'Who are those men out there, General?'

'That's your security,' said the General.

I sat there thinking it over and looking at those boys. And I said, 'General, I don't feel right about all this security. Those boys — what is their security?'

'Their security,' he replied, 'is their training, their arms, and Almighty God.'

'Well,' I said, 'I don't have the training or the arms, but I'll put my trust in God.' And I thought, 'Do I really mean that? Am I ready to go into the dangers of human existence with calmness and peace in my heart, knowing that in life or in death He will take care of me?' I turned to the General and quoted, 'Cast all your anxiety on him because he cares for you.' This is the only real security.

A COMPLETE CHANGE-OVER

An old friend of mine was a salesman. When I first knew him, he was one of the most depressed, defeated, negative individuals I've ever known. He was a lovable fellow but was getting nowhere fast. God had endowed him with a tremendous personality, but it was soft and flabby and had no force behind it. As I got to know him better, I saw that he was afraid. He was afraid of people, of economic conditions, of himself. He tried to cover up this fear with ingratiating sociability. But he didn't get any orders, and even I know that is what you have to do to be a successful salesman. At length, he talked with me about this problem and I prayed with him. All I ever did was to lead him to God. But that was enough, because he went on from there to be successful as a person and successful as a salesman.

SUBLIME ECSTASY

*M*odern science sets up a roadblock to questioning. Even some poetry teaches us that this whole visible universe is but a reflection of vaster realms beyond. The beauty and the loveliness and the charm and the love and the joy of this world are but tokens of that greater world of immortality. Sensitive people become aware of it. For example.

Wordsworth wrote at Tintern Abbey: 'I have felt a presence that disturbs me with the joy of elevated thoughts.'

What is this sublime ecstasy that, even amid common place things, sometimes surges through the human heart and suffuses the whole world with glory? This could very well be a reflection of immortality — that greater, lovelier world intertwined with and superimposed upon this world.

CREATE AN IMMUNITY WITHIN

*N*ever give in! You don't need to, for the Lord God will help you. Follow the 'stick-it-out-and-never-give-up' principle. And keep in mind another idea: the 'keep-God-in-it' principle. No one can be strong, vital, and heroic without the presence of God.

This is a big, overwhelming world and we are small. It is like the prayer the Normandy fishermen offer when they go out on the deep waters to fish. Before they cast off their little boats, they pray, 'O Lord, take care of us. The sea is so vast. We are so small.' And He does and He will.

I tell you from the bottom of my heart: The secret of meeting life victoriously is how close you are to God, how deeply and sincerely you receive Him into your life. And I guarantee you that if you give your life to God, if you commit your life to Him until this becomes your consuming passion, you will have an immunity — not from difficulty, but from defeat. And that is all we can ask.

DOUBT. THINK.

A famous man of letters said that when God wants to make a point with His children, He plants His argument in our instincts; the writer suggests that in deep feelings that cannot be put into words the greatest truths of life are communicated.

I personally had my doubts in my younger days. He who never has to fight a doubt is not a thinker. I sometimes receive letters from parents who are troubled by their children's doubts. A mother will write, for example, that she is worried about her son because he questions everything — he doubts. And I will advise her, 'Thank God for your son's questioning. It means that he is alive, that he thinks. You cannot hand faith down, in packaged form, like an heirloom to your children. They must find it and develop it for themselves.'

When you have to struggle to develop faith, the faith you discover is really your own. It will be a stronger faith if it has had to overcome the pain and struggle of doubt. I can only tell you now that I haven't the slightest doubt about immortality.

THE GREAT DOCTOR

One time I was to speak at a luncheon for a group of professional people. The presiding officer was a doctor. He looked out at the group and said to me, 'If I could reduce the tension and strain under which these people live, I would reduce my caseload. I can't remove those things. But,' he said, 'there is one Doctor who can.' He then quoted from the Bible: 'Great peace have they who love your law.'

Now what is God's law? The laws of nature are a part of it. When Almighty God created us, He knew we could never live as He intended without influences of serenity and beauty and healing peace surrounding us. So in order that our souls might grow great and strong, He set us in a world of great loveliness governed by natural laws. Love God's law, then you will have within you great peace.

LIFE IN IMMORTALITY

In Switzerland, my wife Ruth and I went up to a high valley six thousand feet above sea level, surrounded by the Bernini Peaks. We lingered for only five minutes. But those five minutes will forever remain in memeory. All around us stretched a pristine world, golden sunshine, snow gleaming like myriad diamonds, and a blue sky above. I was so overwhelmed that I didn't even tell Ruth how I felt. But that night I said to her, 'I have today spent five minutes in immortality.'

If mountains an be that beautiful, so can a human being. This is the greatest form of immortality known to us in this life — not the splendour in nature, but spiritual radiance manifesting in man. A strange thing about us: we have evil in us as well as good in us. We have high desires and we have low desires. But Almighty God can change people and bring forth the immortality that is within them.

EMBRACE THE PROBLEM

Consider today a Scripture passage so wise that it contains the answer, or the method for obtaining the answers, to your problems. It is : 'Submit to God and be at peace with him; in this way prosperity will come to you.'

I realize that embracing problems isn't a popular notion. We often encounter an insipid notion that the best thing we can do for people is to free them from all their problems so that they never again have any pain, any difficulty, any hardship, any struggle. Well, no proper-thinking person would adhere to such an idea. Almighty God has made problems an inherent part of the universe — but why? What is He trying to do? What is it all about? He wants to grow strong people: people who tussle with difficulty and grow tough in their minds and in their spirits, the kind of people on whom a great world can be built.

WONDERFUL THINGS ARE HAPPENING TODAY!

These are exciting times! A lot of people grump and whine and keep reminding you that this world is full of trouble. Well, years ago in Syracuse, New York, I.knew a preacher by the name of David Keppel, an Irishman from Belfast. He was almost ninety. I was in my thirties then. One day I was telling him what a terrible state I thought the world was in.

'In Ireland we have a saying,' he explained, '"when there is trouble on earth, it means there is movement in heaven. The more trouble on earth, the more movement in heaven."' Which is a way of saying that the kingdom of God is going to come down out of heaven to replace your troubles in this world.

Who ever lived through more exciting times than these? We see more equality of status among races and expanded opportunities than our ancestors dreamed of fifty years ago. Wonderful things are happening today.

PRACTICE TRANQUILITY

I was impressed by something I read about John Masefield, the poet. He used to perform what he called 'the practice of the getting of tranquility.' Each night he would sit in a chair and repeat to himself, 'This body is a sacred thing. It is the temple of the soul. God created it for my use. God is putting His quietness upon my body.' Then he would put his hand on his heart and say, 'The hand of God is in this hand and I put this hand on my heart. Let not my heart be troubled. I believe in God.' By this time his body would be quiet, free from the quivering tensions of the day.

Next he would say, 'I hereby empty my mind of all jealousy. I hereby empty my mind of all resentment. I hereby empty every impure and evil thought out of my mind. I drain my mind.' And then: 'I now fill my mind with goodness and with love and with forgiveness and with hope.'

With practice, Masefield gained inner peace and achieved victory over tension.

THREE ANSWERS

$\mathcal{I}$ met a lady who said to me, 'I heard your wife make a speech at the church I belong to — and she said something I will always rememeber.'

The woman explained that she had been struggling in prayer for something she wanted and God wasn't answering her prayers. Mrs. Peale, in that speech, remarked that there are three ways God answers prayer: yes, wait awhile, and no. 'And when she said that,' the woman told me, 'I knew I had my anwer. It was no. But I hadn't wanted to take a "no" answer.'

'Maybe that "no" answer is going to lead you to some great experience,' I said. 'Later, on some bright day, you will realize, "If He had not said no, this wonderful thing I now have would not have come to me." '

The attitude that really leads to life in all its fullness is that of a child walking with Him, loving Him, trusting Him, seeking to serve Him. Prayer in this attitude can change your life wonderfully.

SAID MARCUS AURELIUS

$\mathscr{E}$veryone, at one time or another, has been faced with an unsatisfactory situation. The first thing you must recognize is that some unsatisfactory situations cannot be changed; some you just must live with. But the power of God is so great that there is not much need to dwell unduly upon this; it is mentioned merely because one should acknowledge the fact.

The Roman philosopher-king Marcus Aurelius once said, 'Adapt thyself to the things among which the lot has been cast.' Men say these things because they recognize the so-called inevitable difficulties in life. Well, that is heroic indeed. But life would be bleak if all you could do about it was to endure it.

I wish to give you a statement that is worth serious pondering. It is from the prophet Nahum, who said, 'The Lord is good, a refuge in times of trouble. He cares for those who trust in him.' This statement says three things. First, God is good. Second, He protects. You can depend upon Him, no matter what comes. Third, He knows intimately and personally everyone who trusts Him.

YOUR STRONG SHIELD

The Bible says: 'You are my strong shield, and I trust You completely.' That is a tremendous affirmation. I don't know how you begin each day, but here is a suggestion. Instead of rising in the morning and telling yourself, or your wife or your husband, all the difficulties and emergencies you have to face, forget all that and just stand and stretch yourself tall and say, 'The Lord is my strong shield.'

Start the day like that often enough and you will develop composure, confidence, greatness of spirit, understanding, perceptiveness, clear thinking, and the right answers. That is the secret. 'The Lord is my strong shield.'

GET OUT OF YOUR OWN WAY

Do you get in your own way? You might be your most difficult obstacle. To live effectively, you must solve this problem.

Some time ago, I spoke at a convention in Atlantic City. At the end of this meeting, I saw a man whom I have known since we were youngsters. He frequently used to be in my prayers, because he'd become a heavy drinker. After the meeting he said to me, 'I finally got wise to myself. I sure got all fouled up. I messed up years of my life. But that's all gone by now. I finally got wise.'

'How did it happen?' I asked.

'I went back to the church where I grew up,' he told me, 'and I found the Lord and He changed my life.'

This man is now one of the most devoted lay workers for the church in his community. But every time he sees me, he says again, 'What a pity to have wasted all those years! It took a breakdown to get me to where I didn't go on messing myself up anymore.' That is rather uncultured language, but it describes plainly what happens when you get in your own way.

THAT WHISKEY IS NOTHING

I read an article by a doctor about an experience he had had. He was at home when the telephone rang. A man's voice said, 'Will you please come to my house? My wife is having hysterics.' So the doctor drove to this couple's beautiful country home and listened as the wife poured out all her troubles and implored him for something to 'hold on to.' At that moment, the husband came in with three glasses of whiskey and said to his wife, 'This will help your hysterics.' He said to the doctor, 'This will help you too.'

Well, the doctor put the glass on the floor and said, 'This whiskey is nothing to hold on to. Why don't you turn to God?' He sat and talked to them about God. When he left, the hysteria was gone and peace was beginning to come.

When you put yourself into the hands of God, He calms your agitation and upset. You become quiet and are able to handle your problems confidently and intelligently.

AN EMPTY BURLAP BAG

A businessman arrived late to a meeting at our church. He announced, 'I am tense because I was late. I am going to relax the tension in me. In fact, I am going to practice my technique for overcoming tension.'

'How are you going to do that?' I asked.

'I am going to think about God.' He added, 'And I am going to relax my body. I have a rather peculiar practice. I imagine that my body is a big burlap bag of potatoes. Mentally, I take a pair of scissors and cut the end of the bag. All the potatoes roll out, and I am the bag that remains. Now I ask you, is anything more relaxed than an empty burlap bag? I can just feel my whole body falling into complete relaxation.'

There was humour on the man's face, but also dead seriousness. 'I want to live a long life,' he said. 'I feel I have a contribution to make to my country and my God, and I want to be healthy for the long pull. And in order to do it, I must practice relaxation of body, mind, and soul.'

A PLACE OF CALM

*P*ower always comes from a calm centre. Have you ever seen a tornado tearing the sky? I have. It is a sight, believe me! It has astounding force. It can lift up a house and deposit it a mile away. It can take a great board and drive it like a nail through a wall.

The poet Edwin Markham said, 'At the heart of the cyclone tearing the sky …is a place of central calm.' That is to say, a cyclone derives its power from a calm centre.

The human being also derives power from a calm centre. We have to learn how to get rid of tension, how to live relaxed. To do that, acquaint yourself with God and be at peace. I will go so far as to guarantee that if you will commit your life to God, if you will accept God as the guide of your life, and really live this out, you will have no further problems with tension or stress that you can't handle.

The relaxed person is the powerful person. Practice word therapy — serenity, civility, patience, equanimity.

ONE. TWO. THREE.

$\mathcal{I}$ made a list of some of the most enthusiastic human beings I have known. And by analyzing these people, I came up with three essential attributes they all seem to have in one degree or another.

First: These enthusiastic people were very much alive. They were interested in things, concerned, eager. They were sensitive to events and to people and to conditions. They were thrilled by the world, they were excited.

Second: They participated. They gave their whole selves to life. They threw themselves into things.

Third: They all had a deep spiritual motivation that freed them from inhibitions frustrating the free flow of their personality.

Focus mentally and spiritually upon all that is right about life. Because life is mighty good. A lifetime on this wonderful earth doesn't last long, either. It is here today and gone tomorrow. So love it while you can, and you'll be full of enthusiasm.

NEVER LET PROBLEMS WORRY YOU

The other day I was sitting in a luncheon meeting with some business people, and I got to talking about a problem with the man sitting next to me. 'Norman,' he said, 'don't ever let a problem worry you.'

'What do you do, Bob, about a problem?' I asked.

'I do everything I can think of; I give it all I have. Then I put it in God's hands and leave it there. Sometimes, I come up to a fine line where it looks like I'm going to be defeated, but if I put the problem in God's hands, He takes care of it.'

In other words, he was telling me what I am now telling you. Before our meeting was over, the problem was solved in a beautiful way. And as we parted, Bob handed me this note: 'Norman, do you see what happens when you let God take care of things? He moves people a lot better than we earthly guys.' Who says that religion isn't practical? It is the most practical philosophy of human life ever formulated.

LITTLE MINDS. GREAT MINDS.

I came across a passage from Washington Irving's *Sketch Book*. 'Little minds,' he said, 'are tamed and subjugated by misfortune, but great minds rise above it.'

What a picturesque phrase! 'Little minds are tamed and subjugated by misfortune.' But great minds — humanity touched by the glory of God — rise above misfortune. Never accept defeat.

We have cultivated in recent years a 'soft' philosophy — namely, that it is the right and privilege of everyone to be pampered and shielded from the harsh, cruel vicissitudes of human existence. It is true that we are to bear one another's burdens. And it is our duty to care for those less fortunate than we and those who suffer without opportunity. Social awareness, social love, and social service are part of living. But they are not supposed to minimize the fact that a human being should stand in regal, persistent strength and face life heroically.

TAKE TIME

I stopped for lunch with a friend whom I've known for many years. This man is really one of the most inspirational men I have ever known. I greeted him by saying, 'I just met a man who told me it was impossible to be happy anymore.'

'No happiness?' he asked. Then he reached in his pocket and pulled out a card. This is what it said:

Take time To Laugh: it is the music of the soul.
Take Time To Play: It is the source of perpetual youth.
Take Time To Pray: It is the greatest power on earth.
Take Time To Love And Be Loved: It is a God-given privilege.
Take Time To Be Friendly: It is the road to happiness.
Take Time To Give: It is too short a day to be selfish.

I was impressed by this but said to my friend: 'There is one thing left out. I'd like to add it, if you don't mind.'

Take Time For God: It is the way to life.

And it is, too.

WASH YOUR SOUL IN SILENCE

We can reduce the pressure in our lives by the practice of creative silence. Most of us today have no idea how to practice creative silence. But it's a great art, which we all should learn. Rabindranath Tagore, the great Indian poet, said, 'Every day wash your soul in silence.' What a good thought that is!

If you want to master pressure, I would urge you to yield yourself everyday to the silence of God. If we encouraged our young people in this practice, they would develop into more efficient men and women. So I offer the suggestion that in every schoolroom in the land, once, every day, there be a brief silent period. Just plain, non-sectarian silence. I would hope, of course, that some child in this silent period just might start thinking about God. Every family should have a quiet time every day. Everyone in business — or in any place of work — could well have a quiet time each day in his office. Just shut the door, push the papers aside, and be silent. A person communing with the silence will hear right things in it and find new peace.

THE TURNING POINT

A man wrote telling of how he had come through a crisis. 'My left hand,' he said, 'was caught in a rotary mower that was turing at full speed. I clutched my left hand as blood poured through the cotton work glove. I won't even try to recount what happened from that moment on. I got depressed. Life turned flat.'

Then he read an inspirational article by W. Clement Stone on how to draw on your faith when the going gets tough. 'That was the turning point for me,' he declared. 'I said, "Take me over, Lord. Bring what You want out of this." And when I said that, I began to feel a sense of peace and, finally, power.'

What is your difficulty? How painful is it? There is no difficulty that is as big as you are, if you ask for and accept the help of God. God is bigger than any sin, any failure, any difficulty. If you put your life in His hands, you grow along with Him.

INNER ATTITUDES.
OUTER MANIFESTATIONS

Thanks givers are blessing receivers. I believe it is a law of human life that there's a correlation between inner attitudes and outer manifestations. That is to say, what we are within ourselves, we tend to have or create outside us. For example, if your mind is full of hate and resentment and ill will and grudges, you can be sure that you will manifest these things in the life outside your inner soul. We act out what we think. If you're filled with fear, anxiety, worry, and apprehension, you manifest these attitudes so that your life becomes one of fear and anxiety.

By the same token, if in our minds we entertain thanksgiving, we manifest blessings. The more thankfulness a person cultivates, the more he will open to himself the power flow, the vast wealth of heaven. Blessings will pour out upon him.

BE A COMMANDER OF LIFE

*Y*ou can't be a commander of life unless you learn the great art of keeping your head in any crisis. And how is that done? The secret of attaining self-control is the application of practical spiritual principles. The Scriptures are filled with techniques that are so simple that anyone can understand them. And these, when believed in and applied, will in due course give victory over any lack of self-control or lack of calmness.

Here are the steps: When confronted with a big problem, think. Apply all of your mental powers to it. Second, pray for God's guidance, because you will never come out right as long as you think wrong. Third, do all you can do about it. Fourth, put it in the hands of God. Let Him take over and trust Him for guidance and for the outcome. These four principles constitute a basic scientific spiritual formula that will work for the great or the simple.

ALL LIFE IS GROWTH

$\mathcal{H}$uman beings are endowed with a tremendous capacity to grow and to outgrow. All life is growth. The minute a baby is born, he begins to grow. The minute you put a seed in the ground, it begins to grow. Unless you grow, you die. And the secret of growth is to outgrow. The person who has a conscious desire to outgrow can do so by drawing upon his own unused strength.

GOD ALWAYS PAYS HIS DEBTS

*N*o good thing will be withheld from a person who lives a good life. Uprightness means honour, truthfulness, purity, decency — just general goodness. But sometimes we see instances that conflict with our understanding of goodness.

From the early days, we have seen instances where the righteous suffer and bear heartache and pain, while the evil flourish like a tall tree. I've even had people tell me, 'It never pays to be good.' They contend that the smart ones get away with their wickedness, but that good people don't get any reward.

An old farmer once told me, 'God doesn't pay all His debts on the first of January.' And he continued, 'I've watched these evildoers over many years. They may get away with it for one year, five years, ten years, thirty years, maybe forty years. But I've lived a long life, and evil pays in its own coin in the end. Whereas those who are good do suffer, and there is no promise that they won't, they come out on a higher value level.' No good thing is withheld from those who are upright.

WALK WITH GOD

A woman wrote to me saying, 'My husband awoke one morning, drank several cups of coffee, and sat at the table looking so depressed that I couldn't help thinking to myself how very old and dejected he looked. Occasionally he emitted a giant sigh, followed by, "I'm afraid I can't make a go of it. I'm afraid I'm licked." '

She persuaded her husband to repeat affirmations after her. 'He turned to me,' she continues, 'and said, "I feel a little better already." So off he went to work, repeating to himself, "go forth in the name of the Lord." After a few days of this, his shoulders were thrown back and he was breathing deeply of the fresh morning air as he walked to his car. I thought, as I turned from the window, "How alive he is now!" '

Certainly. God is life. This husband had put God out of his life. He was taking only shadows and fear into his life. But when he began to walk with God, new faith cleared the quirks and shadows from his mind and cancelled out his fear.

DO THE RIGHT THING

George Romney, before he became governor of Michigan, was president of American Motors Corporation. At one point, the corporation was almost bankrupt. Everyone was lost in gloom, but Mr. Romney remained hopeful and enthusiastic. He kept telling his associates the situation would turn out all right. One of them asked him, 'But George, what's going to save the company?'

'God is going to save it,' George said. 'God always helps people who are trying to do the right thing.'

So, to recap: Don't get upset, remain calm. Think. And in the name of God, always do the right thing. God always helps people who are trying to do the right thing. The way to put these fundamentals into practice is to acquaint yourself with Him, so that you have His strength, so that you can be at peace. For then you can think and then good will come.

BUILD IT IN YOUR MIND FIRST

A preacher friend of mine came to see me and started pacing the floor, saying, 'I want to describe the church I hope to have some day.' He pictured it all meticulously, specifically, to the smallest detail. He got me so excited that I leaped to my feet, exclaiming, 'The church is already built! It is built in your mind. All you need to do now is finish the job.' Ten years later, I dedicated his church and it was exactly what he had described to me ten years before.

What do you want to build out of your life? How high do you want to go? If you can only think to the rooftop, that is as far as you will go. But you can think your way without limit to the stars. What you are now is what you have been thinking for a long time. What you will be ten years from now depends on what you think from now on. If you want a great life in the future, think great thoughts.

PRACTICE THE ART OF FORGETTING

One of the factors that contributes to mental health is the art of forgetting. Lest you think I rate forgetting too highly, I cite one of the great passages of the New Testament: 'Forgetting what is behind and straining toward what is ahead...'. In other words, turn your back on past mistakes; put them out of your thoughts. One of the wisest book ever written tells you to forget your failures and go ahead.

'Well,' you may say, 'I believe that; but how do you do it?' It is difficult, you say, to put the memory of frustrations and disappointments out of your mind.

Whoever said it was easy? I am only saying it is necessary. If you carry on your mind all the failures and disappointments of the past, lugging them into the future, you'll have too great a weight upon you, and you'll be broken by it.

How then can you forget? My answer is: By will. By positive determination. By disciplining yourself.

ON BECOMING GREAT

We live in an insecure world. Your body is no more secure than your ability to resist disease and infection. Accidents can happen to anyone at any time. This world is insecure. Yet you should never come to the point where you say, 'Life is over for me; I am through. I can't do anything anymore. I haven't any confidence; I have no sense of security.' Remember that the Lord is faithful. He will strengthen you and guard you against all evil. Don't live with too much caution.

It may seem strange that a man would stand in a pulpit and advocate throwing yourself into life, even at the risk of getting hurt. But I have observed that people who try to keep from getting hurt never amount to anything. Only those who throw themselves into risky circumstances — regardless of whether they may get hurt — become really great people. When you live daringly, you do many stupid things; you often make a fool of yourself and people criticize you; and you may fail at one thing and another; but in the long run, you will accomplish great things.

THE WAY THE BALL
BOUNCES...

*A*ll preaching should have practical applications, for religion is a way of life that really works — when it's lived properly. This includes making right decisions. In the long run, you determine what your life will be by your decisions. You can decide yourself into failure or into success, into mental turmoil or into mental peace, into unhappiness or into happiness.

A man remarked to me, 'Let's face it: life goes the way the ball bounces.' I don't go for any such idea as that at all. There is a deeper reality. We can control the bouncing of life's circumstances and outcomes as we learn the art of making right decisions.

And how do we learn it? I repeat: 'If any of you lacks wisdom, he should ask God, ...and it will given.' Believe, really believe, that there is an answer for you and that God will give you the wisdom to find that answer. People who have become great people have been those who have discovered that God will guide them through the problems of their lives.

ENERGIZE EVERYDAY

*W*hat depletes energy? Is it something in the physical being, some malfunctioning, some sickness? Are you tired because you are over-worked? I doubt it. Energy is seldom depleted due to work alone. The factors resulting in losing energy usually originate in our minds. We think tired, depletion, exhaustion, or we nurture hate thoughts, resentment, guilt, or prejudice. These habits siphon off our energy.

If you keep your thoughts alive, clean, and healthy, and if you keep yourself in good physical condition, you can have abundant energy all your life. Almighty God, who created you in the first place, who gave you life, did not finish the creative process at that point. He not only creates; He re-creates. Through Him you can have new life, new vitality, and new energy everyday of your life. In fact, you can possess energy that never runs down.

THE RELAXED POWER

*O*ne day I was working on a sermon. The house was quiet, but I couldn't get the sermon outlined to save me. I finally said to my wife, 'Let's take a walk.'

The ground was covered with deep snow, so we put on our boots and went out. We had our dog Tonka with us. After walking a half mile, Tonka sat down, and Mrs. Peale and I stood beside him. We looked across the valley at the great snow-clad hills. There was not a sound to be heard save the gentle wind in the trees and the singing of the water in a nearby stream — peace, quiet.

After a while, I said, 'Let's go back.' And when we got back to the house, I sat down and had the sermon outlined in about fifteen minutes. Something happened to my whole being when I let go and got out into the harmony and peace of nature where there is power. The secret is to live with relaxed power. When your attitude is easy-does-it, the power can come through.

HOW WOULD YOU FEEL?

J.C. Penney told of how he lived through the Great Depression when he had to face the hard fact that he had lost some forty million dollars. How would you feel if you lost forty million dollars? Well, J.C. Penney became terribly ill and put himself into a sanitarium.

One night, he got the notion that he was going to die. He wrote farewell notes to his family, made his peace with God, and fell into a troubled sleep. But when he opened his eyes and saw sunlight streaming into this room, he realized he had another day of life. He got out of bed, went down the hall and found a group of people singing, 'God will take care of you.'

As he sat listening, he felt two great loving arms go around him, and he knew that God loved him and would indeed take care of him. From that time on he was past being afraid, for he had found the love of God. He regained his health and set about rebuilding his great enterprise.

FIGHT A GOOD FIGHT

*U*nfairness, injustice, hate, pain, sickness, weakness, infidelity — such are the enemies of human beings. Time and time again, a person falters under the onslaught of all this. Sometimes, after you have battled long and been thrown back many times and so many difficulties lie in your path, life throws the whole book at you, and you feel like giving up.

Have you ever felt like giving up? I have. I'd hate to tell you how many times I've felt like giving up. But do you know something? You must never give up. Never. You must fight the good fight. You must finish the course. You must keep the faith. You must never give up. As a human being you must never give up. And if you know this fact, this truth, that God is with you, you never will give up.

MORE BEAUTIFUL THAN A FULL MOON

*B*efore a speech in San Francisco, a man approached me. 'I came here tonight,' he said, 'because I believe in your philosophy that you never need to be defeated.'

And he told me of his own experience. 'Life just ganged up on me, and I felt I was completely through. Finally, I decided I couldn't live that way. So my wife and I started a little programme. Every morning we read the Bible and we prayed. Out of this practice, I got some ideas. And these ideas helped me rebuild.

'I decided I would never accept defeat. Then I decided to start thinking creatively and spiritually. I stopped feeling sorry for myself. I got reacquainted with the God of the new start. Then I got God's directions on how to rebuild.'

There was a full moon over San Francisco that night. It was fresh and clear, and everything was bright and beautiful — but more beautiful than anything else was the look on the face of this man who had decided never to accept defeat.

$\mathcal{I}$'ve heard it said so many times that 'you've got to face the facts.' Take a man of about fifty-five years of age who loses his job and doesn't know where to get another one. A well-meaning friend says, 'Jack, let's face it. When you're fifty-five, it's pretty tough to get another job. You might as well face the facts.' Or consider a couple who got married and raised children but then began to grow apart, and some well-meaning person says, 'Well, you might as well break up. You'll never get together again. You might as well face the facts.'

But in each of these situations, a wise friend should say, 'Yes, this is tough. But be thankful we have a big God, and He will help you to straighten out that situation.' The issue behind the problem is: How much are you willing to trust God? I tell you, friends, I honestly believe that if you trust Him completely, with all your heart, you'll never go wrong. Because He is rightness itself. There is no error in Him. And if you stay with Him, there will be no error in you.

THERE IS A FORTUNE
IN YOUR ATTIC

A newspaper carried an item entitled, *There's a Fortune in Your Attic* that claimed there are several billion dollars in the form of unclaimed securities lying around in old trunks and elsewhere.

Now don't rush out immediately to ransack old drawers; but if I may borrow the phrase, there is a fortune in the form of potential strength, power, joy, and peace in the attic called the human mind.

God who created you told you that He gave you dominion — not over any person, but over the circumstances of life. So don't go on defeated and crawling through life on your hands and knees. We need a new emphasis on the greatness of man. As Wordsworth says, 'Trailing clouds of glory do we come from God, who is our home.' Essentially, man is a tremendous being — a marvellous creature. That means you. It means me. Greatness!

WAS IT A COINCIDENCE?

A missionary's wife in central China during World War II knew the Japanese were approaching her city. She was with her baby girl, two months old, and her son, just over a year old. Her husband had been taken to a hospital, himself ill. He was one hundred and fifteen miles away and would not be back for perhaps a month. The poor woman was filled with fear — she was alone and unprotected, in bitter January weather.

When morning came, she realized that she was without food for her children. She pulled off the calendar page. That day's verse stated simply: 'So then, don't be afraid. I will provide for you and your children'. There was a rap at the door. 'We knew you would be hungry,' said a longtime neighbour, 'and you didn't know how to milk the goats. So I have milked your goats. Here is milk for your children.'

Will you try to explain this away, handle it on an intellectual basis as just pure coincidence? When you come right down to it, what is coincidence? It is an act of God in the midst of time.

WORKING A MIRACLE

$\mathcal{A}$ woman wrote that she had become an alcoholic. One Sunday she saw herself in the mirror — not merely her outward form, but the defeated inner spirit. 'I fell on my knees,' she wrote, 'and cried, "O God, what a mess I have made of myself! Please, dear God, help me."

'Then I got up and sat in a chair. The radio was on and a voice said, "God will help you. Turn your life over to Him. Your life will be different if you do." It really got inside me and I knelt down again and prayed, "Dear Lord, I know the answer. I give You myself, I give You my problem. You take it."

This woman was cured instantly. She lost her desire to drink. Peace came to her, and strength, cleanliness, hope, new life. What do you call such an occurrence? Well, you call it a miracle. It was a spiritual rehabilitation by a power that works when a person really takes it. Real faith works miracles.

'WILL' TO WIN

$\mathscr{A}$s long as you live, no situation is hopeless. As long as you have life and God, and your own intelligence, why should any situation be hopeless? It is because you don't believe in yourself anymore, and you don't really believe in God. Actually, you don't believe in life itself. Start believing and get strength, such as is promised you, from God, who is good.

The statesman Mirabeau, whose clear thinking influenced the course of the French Revolution, once said, 'Nothing is impossible to the man who can will.' I believe that. What is will? It is the determination, the commitment, that you will do something.

'Nothing is impossible to the man who can will.' To have strong will, it must be backed up by faith. So strengthen that will of yours by strengthening your faith. God is good. He is a tower of strength. And He listens to you. So instead of regarding an unsatisfactory situation as hopeless, face it with a will. Then you can change it.

THE GREAT VALUE
OF DISASTER

Governor Charles Edison of New Jersey told me of the time when his father's laboratory at Menlo Park cought fire and burned down. The great inventor was sixty-seven years old, I believe. He stood there, his son told me, watching years of work go up in flames. 'My heart ached for him,' Charles Edison said. 'He was no longer a young man. But then he spotted me and shouted, "Charles, go find your mother. Bring her here. She'll never see anything like this as long as she lives!"'

And the next morning Thomas Edison remarked, 'There is great value in disaster. All our mistakes are burned up. Thank God we can start anew.' Great people do not allow the vicissitudes of life to defeat them. They have something within them that rises victoriously above the losses and disappointments. Whatever comes, life is good. And the thing that makes a person most aware of its goodness is to know God. Leo Tolstoy, one of the greatest men of letters who ever lived, said, 'To know God is to live.'

LIVING WITH QUIET POWER

*H*ow can a person defeat the problem of tension and live with quiet power? Is there an answer? The answer is, 'Blessed is the man you discipline, O Lord, the man you teach from your law.' There is a law by which a person can be organized in his emotional life. It is as certain as the law that lifts the tides. It is not man's law, but God's law. Think God's way, live His way, and you will be freed from tension. You can live with quiet power.

The law of God created you and created me. Every once in a while, you ought to look at yourself and say, 'Think of the complexity of this body with which I am blessed.' And it functions perfectly when kept in harmony with His law. But if your attitudes become contentious, selfish, or hostile — or if you take this wonderful instrument and drive it too hard — then tension, stress, and anxiety takes over. But when you bring yourself back into harmony with God's law, the tension abates and good health returns. The law of God is the law of organization, of harmony, of control.

FINER THAN BEFORE

$\mathcal{I}$f any man is honest with himself, he knows the sin that is in him; he knows the weakness that is in him. And he ought also to know he should confess it to God and ask Him to forgive him and release him from it. And the Lord, who loves him, will respect him for his honesty. So will any good minister respect him. I've had the worst things confided to me by people who conclude by saying, 'You'll never speak to me again. You thought I was a fine person.'

'I think you're finer now than I ever thought you were before, because you have the sincerity and courage to come clean about your wrongdoing and you want to change,' I say to them.

So don't be defeated; don't be weak; don't be wicked. Remember there is the power of God to help you follow through on your prayers. If a person will really pray and will surrender up the evil things that he thinks and does and says, it is incredible what can happen to him.

A WISER WISE MAN

$\mathcal{V}$incent Tracy did more good for alcoholics than almost any man I know. He and I were together for a Christmas night radio programme and he said to me, 'Back in 1948, life and my weaknesses were more than I could take. I started across the Brooklyn Bridge and headed for the Bowery, where I could get a handout. On the bridge I stopped and looked down at the cold water. The uge to jump was strong. But something kept saying to me, "Keep on across the bridge." And over on the Bowery, I suddenly started praying: "Please dear Lord, won't You come to me and help me?" Instantly a great light burst into my mind. I walked away from the Bowery saying the Lord's Prayer, with my hand in the hand of God. And I've been walking along the road with Him,' he concluded, 'ever since. Without Him, I wouldn't be anything.'

'With Him, Vincent,' I said, 'you're a very great deal.' Vencent Tracy was humble enough to be wise. He came to God and became a wiser wise man.

ILLIMITABLE POWER

I read about a young man who suddenly found himself at the top of his class in college, whereas previously he had been rattling around near the bottom. Somebody asked him how he had done this. He replied, 'I went to a handwriting expert who told me I was a natural-born extrovert. When he told me that, on the basis of his science, I was an extrovert, I believed what he said. I began to act like an extrovert. That is why I'm no longer near the bottom of the class.'

You may say this is superficial. It isn't superficial at all. For instance, in the Bible, Paul, in his letter to the Philippians, affirms, 'Christ gives me the strength to face anything.' You have heard that for years. If you really believe it, then you know that spiritually you are a released extrovert. Go out and be that. It is an old and thrilling theme that I just love. No one has ever changed my opinion that a human being has in him illimitable powers. He usually lives and dies without ever bringing more than a tiny fraction of his potential into action.

GREATER THAN
ANY WEAKNESS

$\mathscr{I}$ received a letter from a man who told me that he was just five years old — that he had been resurrected that many years ago. 'I've been around for fifty-one years,' he wrote, 'but I was dead for all but the last five of them.' And he went on to explain, 'Some years ago I was making a good deal of money in real estate, but I started drinking. I lost everything. I became a bum. One day I stopped at the clubroom of Alcoholics Anonymous. I found one of your sermons lying on a table. I stuck it in my pocket and shuffled out. Passing a park bench, I sat down and read that sermon. You said that God was greater than any human weakness. I thought about that and found myself saying, "God, change me!" I went back to my room and slept twelve hours. When I woke up, I was free of my weakness. It was that simple. I am a resurrected person. Once again, I've become a successful businessman.'

A TRUE OPTIMIST

$\mathcal{T}$o be a true optimist, you have to be rugged and tough in mind. An optimist is a person who believes in a good outcome even when he can't yet see it. He is a person who believes in a greater day when there is yet no evidence of it. He is one who believes in his own future when he can't see much possibility in it.

A lot of people live under a cloud. But up above the clouds, the sun is always shining. Down here, on the surface of the earth, groping around in the shadows under a low ceiling, a person may not feel optimistic. But you ought to begin to practice optimism. Send up into the mass of dark clouds bright, powerful optimistic thoughts, a bright optimistic faith. By so doing, you can actually dissipate the clouds and have an entirely different life. Constantly send up into the overcast sky that is blanketing your mind bright thoughts of faith, love, hope, thoughts of God, thoughts about the greatness of life.

IT NEVER RAINS, BUT POURS

$\mathcal{I}$ once spoke with a gentleman who seemed to be on top of the world. His attitude astonished me somewhat, because I knew how much trouble he had been through. You've heard it said, 'It never rains, but it pours.' Well, it really poured on him. But he endured it all, and more than that, he came through victoriously. 'You are a remarkable, indefatigable human being,' I told him. 'You really are something special. How come?'

He grinned and said, 'Years ago, I discovered a philosophy that will stand up under anything. Nothing can break it — and I mean nothing. And it can be stated in five words: Keep believing — never lose faith.'

What a picture! Here is a man who was really up against it and would have folded had he not been able to see that, despite how bad everything was, the goodness of the Lord prevails!

HARD BOIL

$\mathcal{I}$ sometimes read the obituary notices in the papers; the obituaries do not have the romance they once had. When I was a boy growing up in Ohio towns, they used to fill three or four columns. They told the most interesting things about people. From reading those notices you could pick up some wisdom.

Well, some years back, the New York papers carried the obituary of Mrs. Knox of the Knox Gelatin Company. She evidently ran the business herself. She must have been a dynamic and intelligent lady, but rather cryptic, too, and perhaps a bit difficult to work with, for she had a sign in her office warning people about making mistakes. And this is the way it read: 'He who stumbles twice on the same stone deserves to break his own neck.' Well, that is pretty hard boiled. Let us everlastingly be thankful to the good Lord that He has more patience than Mrs. Knox.

THE ONLY WAY...

A man offered to drive me to the airport if I would talk with him about a personal problem. On the way there, he confided all his troubles, worries, disappointments, and unhappiness.

I said to him, 'The only way to free yourself from it is to stand up against it now and practice happiness.'

'How do you practice happiness?' he asked.

I cited the example of John Wesley, who, in his maturity, was one of the greatest men of faith in all the world. At an earlier time in his life, Wesley had no faith whatsoever. So he hit upon the device of acting as though he did have faith. And in due time, he did have faith. You can bring about the ideal condition by persistently acting as though that ideal condition already existed.

'TELL ME WHY...

     One morning after I preached in a church in New Jersey, there suddenly appeared in front of me a woman who bluntly demanded, 'Tell me why I itch all the time.'

I talked with her at some length. It gradually came out that this woman's father had provided in his will that his estate was to be divided equally between his two daughters. Later this woman got the idea that her sister had 'double-crossed' her, and so she built up an enormous resentment and a terrible sense of guilt.

Fortunately, she was a strong person, with the wisdom to insist, 'I am my own sickness. I must get myself healed.' And that is exactly what she did. She took love and forgiveness and goodwill into her; the hatred went, and so did the itching.

Know the truth about yourself and know the truth about God, and you will be set free and become an entirely different person.

IT CAN!

*P*rayer can change your life.

I strongly recommend that you learn the art or science of prayer and put it to work in your life. Now this may seem to you to be just one more religious idea, without much life or sparkle to it. But that is where you would be wrong. It is the way to life itself.

When I say this of prayer I do not speak of the mere mumbling of words. I do not mean formal affirmations either, although formal prayers sometimes help. What I mean is a deep, fundamental, powerful relationship of the individual to God, whereby his whole mind and heart become changed and he receives power from God within himself. I have seen such prayer change the lives of many.

God's peace deeply imbedded in your mind can often have a more tranquilizing and healing effect upon nerves and tension than medicine. God's peace is itself medicinal.

LIVE UNAFRAID

A famous physician has said that fear is the commonest and subtlest of all human diseases. And an equally famous psychologist has declared that fear is the most deteriorating enemy of human personality. Now these men, being scientists, are referring not to normal fear, but to abnormal fear. Normal fear is both proper and desirable. It is a mechanism designed by the Creator for our protection.

Abnormal fear is another matter. If you step over the line that separates it from the normal, you find yourself in a region of grotesque shadows and darkness, obsessions, and mental distortions.

But Almighty God never intended that anyone should live like that, and He has provided an approach by which you can have so much faith that you can live unafraid. There is a power by which you rise above the dangers and uncertainties of human existence and have power over them.

CHANGE!

'Well,' I can hear someone say, 'my trouble isn't that serious. But I'm not a good person. So how do you expect me to step into the new world? I must confess to you, sir, that there is a great deal of sin in my life. I'm weak. I'm a pushover for temptation. I haven't got the strength to give of myself as you say I must in order to enter into this experience. I can assure you that in the depths of my heart I desire it. But what about all these blemishes in my conduct, all these sins, all this hate, all this lust, all this dishonesty? How can I separate myself from these?'

How? By changing, that's all. Anyone can change if he has the desire to change and the will to change and will let God bring about that change.

THE HIDDEN NUGGET

*I*sn't it wonderful to meet a person who is really alive? Not long ago I found myself talking with a man who positively sparkled with vitality. 'Tell me,' I said, 'where did you get so much faith and enthusiasm?'

'I heard you speak at a meeting,' he explained. 'There was something in your talk that day that changed my life. It was a single sentence.'

That sentence was, 'This is the day the Lord has made; let us rejoice and be glad in it.'

'And in what way has this changed your life?' I asked.

'That verse helped me realize that if I take just this one day and do my best, then when night comes I can give thanks to God and go to sleep, knowing that He watches over me.'

Not every day is going to be a pleasant day. Not every day is going to be an easy one. Life brings to each of us some share of pain, struggle, sorrow, heartache. But even in a day that is full of suffering and difficulty, there lies hidden a nugget of something good.

THE TRANSPLANT

$\mathcal{S}$ome years ago, I received a call to come to a hospital to see a patient — a medical doctor. On my way to the hospital, I remembered that a doctor by this name had been mixed up in some crooked business. I went into the hospital room and asked, 'I don't know you, do I?'

'No,' he replied. 'But I know you. I want you to get me out of this place. I have a stomach condition, and it has developed because I hate so many people. I want you to operate on me and get this hate out of me.'

'Doctor, I have a suspicion about you,' I said. 'What have you got on your conscience besides hate?'

After a pause he admitted, 'Doctor Peale, I am absolutely full of rottenness and sin.'

He told me all the dirty things he had done and there were plenty. He wanted to change. And before we got finished in that hospital room, he did just that, for he said to the God, 'I will go with You all the rest of the way.' And he did, too. He got the error out of him and got the truth in him.

FOLLY OF ENTHUSIASM.
INDIFFERENCE OF WISDOM.

*C*harles M. Schwab, one of the great American industrialists, said: 'A man can succeed at almost anything for which he has unlimited enthusiasm.' My friend Raymond Thornburg gave me a wonderful quotation from Anatole France, who said, 'I prefer the folly of enthusiasm to the indifference of wisdom.' George Matthew Adams said, 'Enthusiasm is a kind of faith that has been set afire.'

Sir Edward V. Appleton, the British physicist whose scientific discoveries made worldwide broadcasting possible and won him a Nobel Prize, was asked the secret of his achievements. Now what would you think a scientist of that caliber might say? Well, Sir Edward V. Appleton answered, 'It was enthusiasm. I rate enthusiasm even above professional skill.' It is a fact that people who do not have the skill of the professional, but have enthusiasm that the professional lacks, achieve things. They have the motivational force.

FOCUS ON GOALS

I remember a sign I saw in Syracuse, New York. The winters in upstate New York are rugged, and the spring thaws break up the roads very badly. One spring, near Watertown, I actually saw a sign some farmer had put up that said, 'Choose your rut well. You'll be in it for the next twenty-five miles.' When people get into ruts in living, it's for longer than twenty-five miles. But you don't have to stay in a rut. You can get out of it.

Each of us, I believe, should at intervals re-study his activities and redefine his goals. At times, person ought to appraise carefully what he is doing and ask himself the question, 'Why am I doing this?' We do our work each day, and maybe we do it the best we can. But why are you doing that particular work? What are your objectives, your goals? Could you tell me what your goal is? Or is it fuzzy, hazy? We needs to sharpen our thinking and bring our goals into focus.

WORLD IS A
TUMBLING BARREL

A good friend of mine thinks of the world as 'God's tumbling barrel.' A tumbling barrel is an industrial device for smoothing pieces of metal. It's a revolving drum into which workers put shaped metal pieces that have burrs or rough edges and an abrasive.

The barrel is then rotated. One piece tumbles against another, and the abrasive rubs steadily against them. After some time, the drum is opened, and the pieces are spilled out. The burrs have disappeared, the rough edges are gone. The metal parts are now in shape to function properly in a finished product.

In my friend's mind, this ingenious process suggests the way human beings are tumbled in God's world. As we move through life we tumble against each other and are rubbed by hardships and difficulties. All this friction smooths our rough edges, rounds our personalities, and forces us to use our minds and make ourselves better people.

THE POWER OF CHOICE

An old man from a small New York State community appeared on a national television show. The programme's host was one of the greatest quipsters in the business, but he nearly lost the show to this old man, who was so full of light and fun that he had everybody rocking with laughter.

The host finally said to him, 'Sir, you are the happiest man I ever had on my show. How did you get to be so happy?'

'Why, son,' said the old man, 'every morning when I wake up, I have two choices for the day. One choice is to be unhappy. The other choice is to be happy. So, faced with those two choices, I choose to be happy.'

Now what that happy old man was referring to is one of the greatest powers that you and I possess: the power to choose. By the power of choice, you can either make your life creative or you can destroy it. Somebody said that history swings on small hinges. Similarly, human life develops according to small decisions. We determine our future by our immense power of choice.

SOS

$\mathcal{A}$ man once wrote, 'I was getting near the bottom and couldn't find any way to stop the descent. One day, I went down to the lakeshore and I began to pray. "God," I said, "I need Your help desperately. Please give it to me now. Not later — now." At that exact moment, I was filled with a sense of incredible peace.

'I was forty-five years old. I had never really believed in forgiveness. I carried my sins like a sack on my back. I thought it possible that they might be forgiven, but I couldn't believe they could be forgotten. Now it's as though they had vanished. I feel pounds lighter.'

This is the reason we believe, with all our hearts, in a power that can touch a defeated man and give him power and life again. Believe in God's power, yield yourself to it, and start at once to live differently, in accordance with His will, so that you may be lifted fom defeat to victory, from weakness to strength, and from sadness to joy.

'THIS IS MY DECISION'

$\mathcal{W}$hat we need today is a greater emphasis upon big, strong people. When I was a boy they used to teach us in school that there is a great something a human being can use, which is known as willpower. Later on, a generation of more laid back educators decided this was corny. But they sure produced a corny situation when they abandoned it! The mental health situation worsened when they abandoned stressing willpower.

There is a power in an individual whereby he can decide, 'I will. I will it to be. This is my decision. This is it—with the help of God.' Naturally, willpower is much like whistling in the dark unless you combine it with God's help. But there are rugged people who with God's help take failure or difficulty or disappointment in their stride, extract from the experience whatever know-how it can give them, then relegate it to oblivion. And these people are inspiring.

THE ART OF FORGETTING

A young man came to see me. He had been a teacher in a secondary school. He was highly educated, highly trained, scholastically the best. Naturally when the headmaster retired, he thought he would get the job. But the board brought in a man from the outside. Offended and angry, the young man quit.

I said to him, 'Look, I understand that you are man of great potential and great capacity, but you are ruining yourself with resentment. The thing for you to do is to forget the whole incident. Go back and apply for a position on the faculty.'

Well, he never mentioned it again. He went back on that faculty. Later, when a school needed a headmaster, the board chairman recommended him because he had developed so impressively after mastering the art of forgetting — and he became a headmaster.

What misfortune are you nursing in your mind? Forget it. It's a great art; I've seen many people do it. It's difficult. But it's the way to mastery.

TWO UNEMPLOYED GENTLEMEN

𝒯wo gentlemen I knew suddenly found themselves without jobs. What did the two men do? One said to the Lord. 'I don't understand why this developed, but I know that You have an answer for me.'

Then he made a list of the hundred top executives of great American business organizations. To these men he wrote a letter. He told these presidents exactly what his record was and was absolutely honest. He had seven offers, one of which led him to the very thing in life that he could do best.

The other fellow went all to pieces. And he hasn't made anything of his life even yet, I am sorry to say.

If you adopt the outlook that something great can be done with your trouble, you can do something great. Your outlook determines your future.

GOD OF FAIR BEGINNING

$\mathcal{I}$ wish to remind you of one of the greatest and most helpful facts in this world — namely, that you can start life new every morning. This ought to be comforting for everyone who feels discouraged about yesterday or who thinks the future looks hopeless.

In his poem, *The Song of Diego Valdez,* Rudyard Kipling has a line that is a gem. He refers to 'the God of fair beginnings.' It makes no difference to God what mistakes you've made, what failures you have had. He does not hold them against you. He is the God of fair beginnings. God is big. He forgets, He forgives, He writes it off — because He is fair. No matter how badly things have gone, He always makes it possible for you to make a new beginning.

GOD'S SENSE OF HUMOUR

One of the greatest human beings I have ever known was an old man who lived in Syracuse, New York. One time I went to him for advice about a problem.

He said, 'Well now, son, tell me all about it.' I had no trouble doing that, because my mind was full of it. When I had finished he said, 'You know, God has a sense of humour. You know what He does? When He has a wonderful possibility for you, He buries it at the heart of a big difficulty and He hands you this difficulty. So if you know the mind of God, you thank Him for the difficulty, because you know that, with His exquisite sense of humour, He has buried a bright possibility at the heart of that difficulty.'

'But how do you find this bright thing that has been buried in the difficulty?' I asked.

'You surround the difficulty with prayer and faith and good hard thinking,' answered Mr. Andrews, 'and melt it down. After a while, in the midst of it, you see this bright, shining thing, this potential good.'

YOU ARE NOT ALONE

*B*elieve the great fact that God is with you. And with God's help, what can stand in your way? I have no doubt that you believe in God one way or another, but do you really believe that God is with you, on your side, by your side, in you, helping you? When you have this overwhelming faith in God, when you really believe in Him, and then call upon Him, He will answer and show you mighty things that you never knew.

As you practice this thought, you will become aware that He is also showing you a greater truth. 'Do not be afraid, for I am with you' is probably one of the greatest statements ever made in the history of human life on this earth. 'Do not be afraid, for I am with you.' We are taught this but we do not keep it in mind. Think big. And think the biggest thought of all — that you are not alone, that God will always help you.

IT POSITIVELY WORKS

*E*veryone needs to know how to stand up to a tough situation. The answer to this problem may be given in a concise statement. The one sentence is very simple, but if it is believed in and used, it can help you stand up successfully to any tough situation, no matter what kind it may be. This may seem to be claiming a great deal, but the claim is a valid one. And we find this great truth in the Bible: 'Because you are my help, I sing in the shadow of your wings.'

We can put this truth another way:

Don't struggle so hard. Don't get yourself worked up. Don't fill your life with tension. Do the best you can with any situation and then commit it — that means put it completely in the hands of God, trusting absolutely in Him, and He will bring it to pass in a right and proper manner. This is an old truth, but the wisest and most astute of men and women have believed it, have applied it, and have found that it will absolutely, positively work.

POWER OF THE WORD 'THANKS'

*W*illiam L. Stidger was a distinctive preacher, but at one time he had a nervous breakdown and sat for months in abysmal gloom. He emerged from this by the practice of thanksgiving.

One day a friend said, 'Think of people who have benefited you and ask yourself whether you have ever thanked them.' Stidger gave it some thought, then wrote a letter to an old teacher. Presently he received a letter written in the shaky handwriting of an aged lady. 'Dear Willy,' she wrote, 'I taught school for fifty years. Yours is the first letter of thanks I ever received from a student and I shall cherish it until I die.'

This brought a ray of sunshine into Stidger's mind and he wrote another letter and another and another, until he had written five hundred letters! In the years that followed, whenever depression began to seize him, he would take out his copies of the letters of thanks he had written to people; and the happiness he had felt while doing it would well up in his heart once again.

*H*appiness is not, as some might assume, a light or frivolous topic. Many tend to play down happiness as a superficial objective. But such an attitude is contrary to the facts of human nature. To be truly happy is to be drawing upon the essence of life. Furthermore, happiness fosters healthiness.

A physician once said that happiness corrects imbalances in a person's being. Imbalances, he said, tend to produce sickness, weakness, and deterioration. Balance tends to produce health, strength, and growth. Therefore, genuine happiness brings healthiness.

Happiness will not be found in soft sweetness. It will not be found in moonlight and roses. Happiness in depth — and that is the only kind of happiness that will stand despite trials and continue to be happiness — is to be found through struggle, hardship, pain, suffering, difficulty. It is a joy that is bathed with tears and consecrated by effort. If you are experiencing pain today, look carefully in it for a golden nugget called happiness that has been buried there.

SPIRIT OF FREEDOM

A story is told of an incident during the Nazi occupation of Denmark in World War II. The Nazis told King Christian that they were going to put the Nazi flag on every building in Denmark, saying he could fly the Danish flag beneath the Nazi banner.

King Christian replied, 'If you put a Nazi flag over the Danish flag, in ten seconds a Danish soldier will pull it down and send up the Danish flag.'

'That soldier,' they threatened, 'will be shot.'

'All right,' said the King, 'I will be that soldier.'

They never shot him. Then when they were going to proscribe the Jews and they made them all wear Star of David armbands, the King put a Star of David band on his own arm and protected his Jewish subjects. There are still people who will risk everything for freedom.

TRANSFUSION

*M*any years ago, in a farmhouse in the Midwest, a seventeen-year-old boy was in a coma, desperately ill. The doctor said, 'I see no reason why this boy should die. What he needs is a faith transfusion, a desire to live. In some way he is near death because the faith isn't there to pull him through.' He said, 'If a transfusion like that doesn't happen, he will die before morning.'

When the doctor said that, a farmer drew near and started reading to the boy from the Bible. Hour after hour, he drove those healing thoughts into the boy's unconscious mind until near dawn when, suddenly, the boy gave a sigh. His eyes opened, he looked at the man and at all the people in the room; he gave them a smile and fell into a deep, untroubled, normal sleep.

The doctor checked his vital signs and said, 'The boy will live!' And he did live. Saved by what? By faith and prayer and thought. The problem had its solution right within itself, as all problems do.

THERE IS A CATCH

$\mathcal{I}$ remember an experience of my old friend E. Stanley Jones, the famous missionary. During his first few years in India, he laboured under a heavy sense of personal inadequacy. He began to think he would have to give up his missionary career.

At a meeting in Lucknow he had a remarkable experience. He was praying and he seemed to hear a voice asking, 'Are you ready for this work to which I called you?' Silently, he confessed that he just didn't seem to have the strength. Then the voice said, 'If you will turn it over to Me, I will take care of it.'

But there is a catch. You can't expect God to help you repeatedly unless you help Him. The furtherance of His kingdom on earth comes about through human beings trying to help and serve. That is how He ordained it should be. God wants to have the love and help of people.

FROM IMPOSSIBLE TO POSSIBLE

𝒫ray big. Think big. Believe big. 'According to your faith will it be done to you.' In other words, your life is going to be great in proportion to how greatly you believe. Believe little, you get a little life. Believe weakly, you get a weak life. Believe fear, you get a life of fear. Believe sickness, you get a sick life. Believe big, and you get a big life.

Jesus said, 'Everything is possible for him who believes'. Which means what? That the person who believes is going to get everything he wants? No, it doesn't say that. But it does mean that if you believe big, you move things out of the realm of the impossible into the realm of the possible, you bring to yourself what you believe.

GET THE POWER

*A*re your human relationships what you want them to be? Would you like them to be better? Then why aren't they better? Maybe it is because you fail to realize your full capacity. If all the members of some group of, say, several hundred persons would suddenly realize their full capacity, do you know what they could do? They could change this world. If we would just all catch it!

But how do you catch it? How does one get this power? One thing is certain: you can't manufacture it yourself. Human beings are weak. We are only as strong as we are strong in God. God promises you infinitely more strength. But you've got to reach for it. You have to take it. You have to want it. You have to accept it. Then you have the full complement of power.

GET NEW MANAGEMENT

That happens when a business repeatedly fails to show a profit? Usually it gets new management, doesn't it? A human life that hasn't been going well likewise calls for new management.

Does everything go wrong for you? Why? Poor management. Are you nervous and tense and tired? Why? Poor management. Are you resentful and grumpy and bitter, full of hate and miserable as a result? Why? Poor management. You are making life hard for yourself because you don't think right, you don't act right, you don't plan right. Get your life under new management. Do it by opening your mind and heart to God. Take Him into your thinking and living.

THE CUSTOM OF
SNOW VIEWING

*M*any of us have long since forgotten the romance of the simple basic blessings of this life. A Japanese businessman remarked to me once that his people 'still know how to contemplate and love the simple, basic things of human existence.' He told me of a Japanese custom called a snow-viewing party.

Snow-viewing is usually held on a night when the moon is full, by someone who has a large picture window with a beautiful garden outside. The guests gather. There are no cocktails, there is no hubbub, no empty conversation, no hand-shaking. You sit and look through the picture window at the snow, at the stark, bare trees with little flecks of snow on them, at the great rocks capped with snow. You spend an hour or two, in silence, viewing the snow and thinking and meditating. Then you rise, bow, and go home. That is all, but you have had an hour of quiet fellowship with sensitive, appreciative people. Life is good; and you walk along thinking long thoughts about how lovely the world is. So let us give thanks for the deep basic things of human existence and for family, friends, and loved ones.

THERE IS ONLY ONE RULE

*A*fter two years of professional baseball with the St. Louis Cardinals, Frank Bettger hurt his arm and had to give up baseball. He spent two years in a dismal job, then he switched to selling life insurance. His first ten months in this new work were the most discouraging months of his life. He would make many calls without selling a single policy.

Finally, Bettger decided to 'burn up the paths' in life insurance, just as he had done in baseball. The next day, he sold a policy to his first prospect. That was the beginning of a spectacular career. Insurance people tell me that Bettger is regarded as having been one of the greatest salesmen in the history of life insurance. And on the subject of developing enthusiasm, Bettger says, 'There is only one rule. To become enthusiastic, act enthusiastic.

Practice enthusiasm in even the most commonplace things and presently the immense power of enthusiasm will begin working wonders for you.

IT IS LIKE MUSIC

A young man told me his grandmother was always doing good. I decided to look her up. After finding the house, eventually I saw an elderly lady coming down the road, carrying a big basket on her arm. And she was singing — beautifully and melodically — at the top of her voice.

'Are you Mrs. Wright?' I asked.

A big smile crossed her face as she said, 'Of course, that's who I am. What do you went to see me about?'

'I had a letter from your grandson and he says that you are an angel on two feet,' I explained. 'Please tell me how you got to be so happy.'

'I just love everyone,' she answered. 'When you have the God in your heart, you love everyone and it's like birds singing. It's like music all day long.'

INDIVIDUALS CAN OVERCOME IMPOSSIBILITIES

*P*eople talk about the evils of our society — the breakdown of morality, the rising incidence of crime, the growing paganism of our generation, and the dishonesty rampant in human affairs.

Sometimes people say, 'It's so bad that you can never do anything about it. These things are so deeply rooted in the wickedness of human nature that you can never eradicate them. It's an impossibility.'

It is my humble judgment that the remedy for these social impossibilities is for individuals to be so stimulated and motivated, to become so identified with God, that they become part of His process of overcoming impossibilities.

'Here I stand; I can do no other,' said Martin Luther. It was he himself, individually, who stood for principles so forcefully that he initiated great changes in the social order. Individuals overcome impossibilities.

WHO MADE THIS WORLD?

$\mathcal{Y}$ou may say, 'You don't know the difficulties I have. There are so many problems. I have inner conflicts and all kinds of trouble. Yet you tell me not to be depressed.' But let me ask you: Would you want all those problems and troubles to be taken away from you? Who made this world? Some whimsical being? Some devilish individual? Or was it someone with wisdom? You know it was someone with wisdom because everywhere you find order and law; and wherever you find order and law, you are beholding signs of intelligence. This world was created by an intelligent God. He put you in it, and He put some trouble in it along with you. Why? Because He wants to make a great person out of you. If He didn't care whether you ever amounted to anything, He wouldn't have put any difficulty in your life.

GET ABOVE DISCOURAGEMENT

$\mathcal{D}$iscouragement is one of the most pernicious diseases of the human spirit. It weights heavily upon the mind, making its judgments grotesque and unsharp. It saps energy. It destroys creative possibilities. It renders us ineffective.

And let's face it, oftentimes there is much cause to be discouraged. If I wanted to, I could give you quite a talk on all the things you might find to be discouraged about. But I don't think it's my job to tell you how bad things are. You know that already. My theme is that you can do something about it. You can learn to handle and get above discouragement. Out of discouragement, rightly handled, great things come.

THE OBSESSIVE BELIEF

I've observed one thing that has never ceased to impress me. The person who has a certain great truth in his mind can never be defeated by anything and will ultimately win victories, though he may have to go through the deep waters now and then. That great truth is the belief — the obsessive belief — that God is always with us. When you believe this, you are not alone, never, under any circumstances. When you live with this belief, you are never rejected, you are never forsaken, you never walk by yourself. God is with you — this is the greatest source of strength a human being can have.

GREAT TO BE ALIVE!

We need to recall and give thanks for the gift of life itself. We're so accustomed to being alive that we take it for granted. The thrill and the wonderment of it elude our minds. Do you ever get up in the morning and look out the window or go to the door and breathe in the fresh air and go back in and say to your wife or husband, 'Isn't it great to be alive?' Probably if you did, your spouse would have a heart attack! But life in itself is so tremendous, such a privilege, that it should be cause for deep thanksgiving.

YOU ARE FREE

God is so big that He has confidence in His creatures. He gives them the power of private judgment; He makes them free moral agents so that they can do what they want to do — even contrary to His will. That is a big God. If God were a little god, He would tell us exactly what to do. But He leaves us free.

You and I repeatedly make a mess of things — that's for sure. To some people, the human picture looks quite hopeless. Life is dark at times. But I hold with the faith expressed by John Greenleaf Whittier in the lines:

> I know not where His islands lift
> Their fronded palms in air;
> I only know I cannot drift
> Beyond His love and care.

Beyond this universe, is eternal goodness. The conflict between evil and good, between hate and love, goes on and on; but love is fundamental and underlies the immortality of the soul.

FORMULAS FOR SUCCESS

*S*am Reeve was so poor that the first time he ever wore a suit was the day he graduated from high school, and the suit was given to him by a neighbour. One day, he read this passage in the Bible: 'Give, and it will be given to you. A good measure, pressed down, shaken together and running over, will be poured into your lap. For with the measure you use, it will be measured to you'. Sam decided to predicate his life on this and eventually became an outstandingly successful small businessman. He was invited to a White House conference of small businessmen who had done distinguished jobs. The president asked him, 'Sam, how did you do it?'

Sam thought a moment and then answered, 'I just tried to give away more than my competitors. I try to find my pleasure in giving,' he said, 'and let the getting part take care of itself.' I tell you, if you really believe in God, you've got to believe in this. If you want a life full of blessings, a life out of poverty, a life victorious over difficulties, if you want things to flow your way, you practice that.

CAN I UNLOAD MY MIND?

$\mathcal{G}$od knows that human beings need help. No matter how strong they may be or what attainments they may have to their credit, they are still faced with many problems that upset them. Even though their faces may look calm and peaceful, people may be upset to one degree or another.

Only a short time ago, a man came to my office whose name I think would be known to nearly everyone who has any knowledge of the American business world. He manages a vast industrial empire. He is one of those men born to leadership, a strong, powerful character. And he sat in my office and asked me, 'Can I unload my mind to you?'

'Go ahead,' I said. And he was with me for a long time, for he had lots to unload. There he sat in front of me, a powerful, famous man, but at the same time just a human being whose mind was terribly upset. He had come to talk with me because he wanted me to tell him how God could help him. I was touched. And he was touched. And he was helped.

GIVE... AND GIVE GENEROUSLY

Through extraordinary intelligence, hard work, and by the application of the basic laws of successful achievement, W. Clement Stone has made huge sums of money. But I never knew a man who gave so much money so generously as does Mr. Stone. It appears that his chief reason for making money is to help people. For example, he has helped more prisoners to find new life — and more boys to find a future — than anyone I know of. He started life with nothing. He said that the Lord just gave him the gift of making money.

But I've noticed that a lot of people who make money hang on to it. Some of the tightest people I've ever known are people who have made money — they've got the idea that it is for them alone. If you have the ability to acquire wealth, you should learn the equally important art of how to give it for mankind. You are a steward of God, who made everything and owns all values of this world.

GIVE ANYWAY

Frank Boyden was headmaster of Deerfield Academy at Deerfield, Massachusetts, for over sixty years. When he first took charge, the Academy was heavily in debt. But if you go there today, you will see the most marvellous campus. I asked Frank Boyden one day, 'How did you get this place built up?'

'Whenever I got to rock bottom,' he said, 'I'd talk to the Lord about it. The Lord would say, "Frank, give some more." I would tighten my belt and give more of my own money, more of myself. And the blessings have just rolled in — because I wanted to make good men out of little boys and I gave of myself to do it.'

I will tell you this: If you are missing blessings in your life, if the flow of prosperity has been inhibited, the thing to do is start giving! Even when you haven't anything to give, give anyway. This is what is offered to you through the law of supply. The law of supply works only as long as you give.

DON'T PRAY LIKE A CHILD

*P*rayer is a mental process. Oftentimes a person will complain, 'I've prayed and prayed and I didn't get what I wanted.' You didn't?

Well, who said you were supposed to get what you wanted? Prayer isn't a device to get you what you want. Prayer is a means of bringing you to the point where you will accept what God wants. If you're using it just for getting what you want, you're engaging in an improper and degraded use of it.

The Lord does want good things for us all, and if with all your heart you pray for something that is wholesome and constructive, you are likely to receive it. But sometimes the thing you pray for is something you shouldn't have.

We are like children — we want what we want when we want it. But to be a mature person you have to learn to say, 'This is what I'd like to have, Lord, if You think it's all right for me, but if You don't, then give me what You want me to have or show me what You want me to do.'

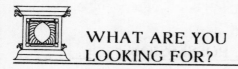

WHAT ARE YOU LOOKING FOR?

W. Clement Stone is a philosopher who says that God wants to do wonderful things for you. You get exactly what you are looking for, he says.

If you seek inspiration, you become inspired. If you seek knowledge, you become informed.

If you seek wisdom, you become wise. If you seek health, sickness disappears. Seek good and it comes to you. Seek success and it will come to you. Know specifically what you want and then keep your mind on that which you want — and off the things you don't want.

If you keep thinking about what you don't want, you'll get what you don't want. But if you think about what you want, it is likely to come to you.

*W*hen an old friend's last will and testament was read, it contained the following declaration:

'I desire to testify and give thanks for: the goodness of God, who has blessed me far beyond my merit; godly parents; the patience and devotion of my wife; the noble character, love, and loyalty of my darling daughter, my son-in-law and their family, and my grandchildren; the rich fellowship of my friends; the kindness and co-operation of those with whom I have been associated in business; the opportunities for service in the community and in the church; the strength for daily toil; the joy of living; the inexpressible reward of striving, even in an imperfect way, and the glorious certainty of life eternal and abundant. These comprise my real possessions.'

My friend had so many blessings because he was constantly activating the flow of blessings by giving praise and thanks to the Source of it all.

THE GREATNESS WITHIN

*C*he Empire State Building is a marvellous structure. Seeing it reminded me of a boy who lived in downtown New York City in devastating poverty. At the age of thirty, he was elected to the New York State Assembly and was assigned to the committee on banking; he had never had a bank account up to that time. He was so discouraged trying to read the bills that came before him that he almost decided to quit.

I am talking about Alfred E. Smith, four-time governor of New York. And he later realized his dream of building the tallest building in the world, the Empire State Building. Once I sat with him in that building and said, 'Governor, you have had a great career. Tell me about it.'

He smiled and replied, 'My mother always believed in me. She said there was something in me that God would bring out if I allowed Him to do so.'

So if you are not satisfied with your life, say, 'Lord, help me to bring out the greatness that is within me.' What God can make out of a person is astounding.

UNLOCK THE FLOW OF POWER

Ernest L. Wilkinson wrote a booklet on tithing, and one day we got to discussing the subject. He said, 'The way to unlock the flow of power is to give.' And he told me about a man in Grand Rapids who made furniture.

This man got into difficulties and practically went broke. He was able to save the factory, but his credit was thin. The banks wouldn't loan him money, so a few friends loaned him enough to get started again. Then he got the idea of tithing — giving ten per cent of his income and his time to the Lord. When he was ready to start his factory again, he knelt in his office and said, 'Lord, this plant, such as it is, is Yours. I accept You now as my partner and I will give the first ten per cent all the rest of my life to You.' His business grew and he brought blessings to other people.

The basic spiritual law of the universe, is that blessings come form giving yourself away. If you can believe this, all things are possible.

FACE YOUR PROBLEMS

We encounter some real troubles in life. Anyone living on Earth will know of someone who is having a grievous time with real troubles. I think there are certain basic things we can do when we're in trouble to keep our troubles from overwhelming us.

The first is to remember God and have faith in His providence. Look to Him for guidance. And from this there follows a second basic idea: Since we are children of God and can look to Him for help, we ought not to quake in the presence of trouble, nor run away from it, nor pretend it isn't there — but face it, stand up to it, take hold of it, and deal with it. Actually, the more you try to run away from trouble, or evade it, the more overwhelming it becomes; while if only you would boldly take hold of it, you would find it that much easier to handle.

TESTING TIMES

*W*hen I was a boy, several people told me they didn't think I would be able to make much of anything out of my life. So I was comforted to read an article by Alston J. Smith in which he mentioned a number of distinguished men and women who early in their lives had been the butts of brutally discouraging remarks — including Thomas Edison and Louisa May Alcott.

One of the functions of a temple, mosque or church is to help people who have lost faith in themselves, who are overcome with difficulties and problems, by reminding them who they are. There isn't anyone who hasn't within himself tremendous possibilities. You should never let the fact that you have problems and difficulties overcome you. If you have a whole armful of difficulties, you may be sure the Lord likes you. And He knows that you have what it takes to dig down into this difficulty and that problem and come up with bright and shining good:

IN A WORLD FULL OF TROUBLE

*S*ome people seem to be afraid to partake of any optimism put to them — as though there were something blasphemous about taking a hopeful view. Pessimism thrives, the intellectuals say, because the world is in so much trouble. Certainly it's in trouble. When hasn't it been in trouble? This is the nature of human existence. The bright fellows who think they are going to create a perfect world have a superficial understanding of the nature of life. It always has been a world full of trouble and it always will be. But out of this world of touble rise people who live above the trouble.

What is your trouble? It isn't anything you can't rise above. Not by your own strength, but with Him lifting you. There is an old song in which each line of the refrain ends, 'He lifted me.' Get lifted in the spirit, and life will have great new meaning.

PARTICIPATE IN LIFE

*W*hen an individual really is enthusiastic, you can see it in the flash of their eyes, in their alert and vibrant personality. You can see it in the spring of their step. You can see it in the verve of their whole being.

Enthusiasm makes the difference in our attitude toward other people, toward a job, toward the world. It makes a great big difference in the zest and delight of human existence. Do you have enthusiasm? Or have you grown dull? Lackadaisical? Indifferent? Has the zest gone out of you? Well, remember that a person can gain an enthusiastic participation in life.

Enthusiasm lifts living out of the depths and makes it mean something. Play it cool and you may freeze. Play it hot and even if you get burned, at least you will shed warmth over a discouraged and bewildered world.

HEAVENS ARE FALLING

On his early life, Abraham Lincoln travelled the court circuit and stayed overnight, as was his custom, with an old Illinois farmer. One night the farmer witnessed the spectacular phenomenon known as 'shooting stars.' He thought the end was at hand and he got scared. Then he remembered Lincoln was asleep upstairs. He dashed up the stairs crying, 'Abe, Abe, get up! The heavens are falling! The world is coming to an end!'

Lincoln got out of bed and looked out the window. He stepped back into the room, put his hand on the shoulder of his frightened friend, and said to him, 'Don't you be afraid, Bill. Even if there are some shooting stars, the great constellations are still there.'

When difficulties rain down upon you, it is easy to become bewildered and frightened. But if you look behind the difficulties into the eternal verities and see that the great God is still there, then you realize you need not be afraid. Because of His presence, you have what it takes to face up to anything.

The Bible is filled with astonishing passages. One of them can be found says, 'What is impossible with men is possible with God.' Now, of course, on the surface this means that God can do things man cannot do, which is a fact that goes without question. But it seems that this verse implies that if people are identified with God in a special way, the power of God to change impossible into possible becomes associated with those people. This, of course, is an enormous assumption. But the Scriptures deal in enormous assumptions.

You, too, have it in you, as do I, to do (using an ordinary phrase) the things that cannot be done. But there is a tendency in human nature to emphasize the seemingly impossible in life, to underscore them, to build them up. This is one reason why the life accomplishment of many of us falls at a far lower level than God ever intended it to be. To the degree that we identify ourselves with Him, we gain power over the seemingly impossible.

LIVE LIFE

*A*re good people happy people? They're on the way to being happy. They've made the start. They've gone down the road a long way, but they'll not have power that brings deep joy until they penetrate the essence. I fervently pray that this might happen to us all. Let us go deeper through self-surrender, through self-giving, through desire, through earnestness, until the glory bursts upon us and true happiness surges up and fills our lives.

Did you ever stop to ask yourself how alive you are? God, who breathed into us the breath of life, certainly intended that a person should have fullness of life. What a pathetic thing it is that some people seem to live out their days without ever being fully alive! The greatest gift outside of the salvation of our souls is the gift of life itself. And the salvation of our souls is life eternal.

YOU CAN ACCOMPLISH IMPOSSIBLE

*C*an people do impossible things? Of course they can. We are constantly witnessing demonstrations of humankind's immense power to do what was once considered impossible.

Some foolish people believed it was irreligious for anyone to go beyond the atmosphere of the earth. But it's all God's universe. When astronauts venture into space, they find natural laws like the ones we encounter on earth. God rules the universe with law.

But have you noticed that the almost impossible is carried out by men and women who are poised and fearless? Naturally, to get people who can do the impossible, you have to get people who are identified with God. Only God can do impossible things, and only a man or woman of God can share with Him in the accomplishment of the impossible.

Secrets of Success

Charles Newton

Rs 50.00

When was the last time you tried to punch a hole in the sky?

Tests Pilots, punching into stratosphere, climbing to undreamt heights in jets and rocket planes, have a phrase they use to describe their work.

They call it ' punching holes in the sky. '

That is what we are meant to do with our lives, to climb beyond the humdrum, to reach beyond the preoccupation of daily existence. However, more often that not, we aim too low. When it comes to living we settle for the mediocre. We are human, we tell ourselves. The sky is too high to think of. It is the impossible that stops us. But nonetheless it is the challenge of the impossible that gets life out of its rut and onto a highway that leads us to our goal.

Think big, work hard and have the courage to dream. Make the impossible your goal.

Remember, if you don 't care for your dreams, who will.

Whatever your personals goals, this book will help you become the person you have always wanted to be.

' ... a delectable book which in irresistible prose lays down the keys to success. '

Amrita Bazar Patrika

Available at all bookshops or by V.P.P.

Orient Paperbacks

Madarsa Road, Kashmere Gate, Delhi-110 006